M000194383

Tom Packer

Rusty Cassway

Mike Dudas

Brian Sullivan

"I'll hold the light babe" (Bert Malcolm)

YOU ARE THE EXPLORERS OF THE DEEP
— Greg Masi

This book is not a mystery novel. I did not write it in that form, with clues, false leads, red herrings, and a revelatory climax with a twist ending. In form, this book is more of a research procedural. It is not about an unidentified perpetrator who meets a just fate. There is little justice in the real world, in which the perpetrator goes free while his victims remain dead, buried, and for the most part neglected or forgotten.

This is not to say that a great deal of detective work was not required in order to achieve an ultimate conclusion. In that sense, this book is about what the police call a "cold case:" one that was never solved and remains open on the books.

This crime occurred in 1942. Its case was not solved until 2018: seventy-six years after its commission.

To skip to the chase: Sean Manni discovered a shipwreck; Rusty Cassway identified it. "It" is the steamship *Octavian*, torpedoed by a German U-boat during World War Two.

How these situations were set in motion, what predicaments resulted, and what circumstances eventuated, are subjects of the present volume. The tale is long and convoluted, filled with side trips that set the pace for a group of individuals known as "wreck-divers."

This is their story.

Research Vessel *Explorer*

FIFTEEN CENTS   FEBRUARY 2

TIME

THE WEEKLY NEWSMAGAZINE

Vuk Vuchinich

GERMANY'S U-BOAT VICE ADMIRAL: DOENITZ
His victories are in Davy Jones's locker.

The architect of the wolf pack tactic was Vice Admiral Karl Doenitz, shown here on the cover of *Time* magazine for February 2, 1942: two weeks before Reinhard Hardegen, skipper of the *U-123*, torpedoed and sank the *Octavian* with the loss of her entire crew.

Paukenschlag, Hardegen,
and the
SS *Octavian*

by **Gary Gentile**
with much help from **Rusty Cassway**

Gary Gentile Productions

Copyright 2020 by Gary Gentile

All rights reserved. Except for the use of brief quotations embodied in critical articles and reviews, this book may not be reproduced in part or in whole, in any manner (including mechanical, electronic, photographic, and photocopy means), transmitted in any form, or recorded by any data storage and/or retrieval device, without express written permission from the author. Address all queries to:

Gary Gentile Productions
500 Lehigh Gorge Drive
Jim Thorpe, PA 18229
gary@ggentile.com

Additional copies of this book may be purchased from the same address by sending cash, check, or money order in the amount of $20 U.S. for each copy (plus $4 postage per order, not per book) in the U.S. Inquire for shipping cost to foreign countries). Alternatively, copies may be ordered from the author's website and paid by credit card:

http://www.ggentile.com

Picture Credits
All uncredited photographs were taken by the author. The front cover photographs were from *"Auf Gefechts=Stationen!"* (1943), by Reinhard Hardegen. The top photograph shows the *Culebra* sinking. The photograph below it shows *Culebra's* survivors in a life raft as they approach the *U-123*, before being abandoned at sea. The bottom photograph shows an unidentified U-boat. The back cover photographs show the *Octavian* topside (courtesy of Rusty Cassway) and the *Octavian* underwater (photo by Rusty Cassway), the latter depicting the engine and boilers where the builder's plaque was discovered. This plaque led to the identification of the wreck.

International Standard Book Numbers (ISBN)
1-883056-55-1
978-1-883056-55-1

First Edition

Printed in U.S.A.

Contents

Introduction – Those Who Seek . . .

Here is the short version:

On June 30, 2018, Sean Manni – skipper and owner of the *Jersey Dragon* – embarked on a three-day dive trip off the coast of Maryland. The purpose of the trip was to dive on a number of hangs in the hope that they might be shipwrecks. This kind of trip was always chancy. Instead of diving on known locations in order to be certain of exploring a shipwreck, and perhaps catching a few lobsters, they might dive on nothing but rock piles and junk heaps: a poor return for their time, effort, and money.

But, as I have often said, "Only those who seek, will find."

And find they did. Sean was lucky – and I use the word "lucky" loosely, considering the time, effort, and money that was invested in making the discovery. He hooked into a large steel wreck that was loaded with brass portholes. He and his fellow divers recovered five of them. In addition to Sean, also aboard on the discovery dive were Ryan Cooling, Kevin Kohling, Harold Moyers, Andy Skapik, and Evan Skapik.

The following afternoon (July 30, 2018), after the boat returned to the dock, Sean posted on Facebook a series of photos that showed the recovered portholes. This posting alerted the dive community not only of the great success of the *Jersey Dragon's* search trip, but of the existence of a previously unknown steamship that had the potential to yield additional artifacts.

One person who took advantage of the discovery was Rusty Cassway. He wasted no time in calling his and Sean's mutual friend Bill Cleary. The two of them talked on the phone for more than an hour. As a result of this conversation, Rusty inferred the approximate area in which Sean had been searching, but not the specific location. Bill Cleary did not know the exact location, but he knew from talking with Sean that the depth was 188 feet.

Rusty examined his list of hangs. He did not have this list by accident. He had accumulated hang logs for years, then paid a couple of secretaries $15 per hour to type the numbers into a database. The result was a database that contained more than 29,000 sets of hang numbers. He found a cluster of hangs at a depth of 190 feet in the approximate area in which he thought Sean had found the unknown steamer.

Rusty Cassway and his partner Brian Sullivan, owners of the dive boat RV *Explorer*, plus Mike Dudas and Tom Packer, departed from Cape May, New Jersey on July 4, 2018, and headed for the cluster of hangs at 190 feet. They were in luck – and I use the word "luck" loosely, considering how much time, money, and effort went into creating the hang log database – and found the same wreck that Sean had found several days earlier.

As luck would have it – again I use the word "luck" loosely, for luck favors the prepared mind – Rusty found and recovered the ship's brass builder's plaque between the engine and one of the two boilers.

The builder's plaque was not embossed with the name of the vessel, but with

the name of the ship builder, the city of construction, and the serial numbers of the engine and boilers. This meant that Rusty had to do some research in order to identify the wreck. He accomplished in days what would have taken months or years in pre-Internet times. Because the words on the plaque were written in Norwegian, Rusty contacted the Norwegian Maritime Museum in Oslo, Norway. In a trice, museum historians found that the numbers on the plaque correlated with company documentations for a vessel called *Octavian*.

According to the history books, the *Octavian* was lost with all hands after being torpedoed by the *U-203* on January 17, 1942. But there's a catch: according to German records, the *Octavian* was sunk off the coast of Newfoundland, hundreds of miles from where the wreck lay on the seabed.

After Rusty contacted me, I went through my personal library and found some obscure footnotes which stated the possibility that the *Octavian* may instead have been sunk by the *U-123* during Paukenschlag (as the initial round of U-boat attacks against the American coast was called in Nazi Germany). I suggested looking at the deck log of the *U-123*. The deck log, or KTB (Kriegstagebücher), could be found on microfilm in the National Archives at College Park, Maryland. I also advised him that the log would be in German.

At the moment of sending that email to Rusty, I completely forgot that I possessed copies not only of the original log in German but of an English translation. I had used the log entries in writing *The Fuhrer's U-boats in American Waters* (2006).

By the next morning, my mental fog had dissipated. I went to the filing cabinet that held archival information on U-boats that had operated in the Eastern Sea

Frontier during World War Two (the subject of *The Fuhrer's U-boats in American Waters*). I pulled out the folder for the *U-123*, and read how the skipper described the sinking of a freighter off the coast of Maryland, on the very night on which the *Octavian* was listed in the German records as having been sunk by the *U-203* off Newfoundland.

I called Rusty at once, but I was too late. Because Mike Dudas worked for Rusty, Rusty had already informed him of my original finding. Ever the go-getter, Mike had wasted no time in locating on the Internet an English translation of the *U-123's* deck log. He had already shared it with Rusty. That meant that all three of us were literally on the same page.

Rusty told me that the location that was given on the U-boat's deck log was only 800 yards from the wreck site.

Thus in one fell swoop, not only was the shipwreck positively identified, but the history books were corrected about which U-boat was responsible for sinking the *Octavian*, and where. And all this in less than a week. I wish that all shipwreck discoveries and identifications were so easy.

But that's not the end of the story. Rusty cleaned and conserved the builder's plaque to its original polish, then made arrangements with the Norwegian Maritime Museum to travel to Norway in order to donate the plaque for permanent display in the museum.

The official plaque donation ceremony was scheduled to take place on May 8th, 2019. This was the date of an annual event in which Norway celebrated her day of liberation from Nazi Germany in 1945. Invited to this major event were the heirs and descendants of those who lost their lives when the *Octavian* was torpedoed and sunk, thus connecting some of "those who seek" with families who for many years have agonized over the fate of their brave seafaring relatives who disappeared on January 17, 1942. Those who questioned, now have answers.

What follows is the long version. Keep in mind that those who seek are also those who dare.

The *Octavian* looking crisp and clean. (Courtesy of Rusty Cassway).

C1 - A Brief History of the *Octavian*

Built: 1938	Sunk: January 17, 1942
Previous names: None	Depth: 188 feet
Gross tonnage: 1,335	Dimensions: 250' x 41' x 14'
Type of vessel: Freighter	Power: Oil-fired, two-cylinder steam turbine

Builder: Nylands, Verksted, in Oslo, Norway
Owner: A/S Rederiet Julian (Hilmar Reksten, manager)
Port of registry: Bergen, Norway   Radio call sign: LJXS
Cause of sinking: Torpedoed by *U-123* (Kapitanleutnant Reinhard Hardegen)
GPS: 38-00.469   74-21.326

What's in a Name?

Octavian is a name that goes far back in history.

Perhaps the most famous person who is known by that cognomen was first called by his birth name, Gaius Octavius Thurinus. He lived between 63 BC and 14 AD (77 years). When Octavian was adopted by his great-uncle, Julius Caesar, he changed his name to Gaius Julius Caesar. After Julius Caesar was assassinated in 44 BC, Octavian joined with Mark Anthony and Marcus Aemilius Lepidus to form the Second Triumvirate of the Roman Empire.

My readers should understand that leaders in those days were not elected by the populace. They elected themselves by means of assassination, bloodshed, and torture. Although Julius Caesar is remembered largely as the Roman general who expanded and consolidated the Roman Empire by conquering Gaul and Britain, then later became dictator of the empire, he was one of the most bloodthirsty perverts in history. There is no telling how many people he personally murdered, or how many he had tortured, raped, and put to death. His military campaigns included the wholesale massacre of civilian populations. In short, he was a modern-day Adolf Hitler.

Julius Caesar's nephew was not much better. His first order of business after assuming power subsequent to his uncle's death, was to track down and kill everyone who was involved with his uncle's demise. This included the murder of everyone who had supported the downfall of Julius Caesar, all of Octavian's political opponents to the throne, and potential future enemies.

Octavian also continued his uncle's campaigns of conquest, adding materially to the size and strength of the Roman Empire by conquering Hispania, and by taking military possession of Dalmatia (today, parts of the countries of Albania, Bosnia-Herzegovina, Croatia, Kosovo, Montenegro, and Serbia), Egypt (and other parts of North Africa), Noricum (today, parts of Austria and Slovenia), Pannonia (today, Hungary and parts of Austria, Bosnia-Herzegovina, Croatia, Servia, Slovakia, and Slovenia), and Raetia (today, parts of Austria, Baden-Wurttemberg, Bavaria, Germany, Italy, Switzerland, and Vorarlberg). All these countries and tribes became unwilling provinces of the Roman Empire.

Again, there is no way to count the number of defenders who were killed in battle, or how many additional men, women, and children were tortured, slain, or executed out of hand. Roman legionnaires often killed just because they could.

Keep in mind that the word "conqueror" connotes if not directly equals "mass murderer." I was never told this in school. I was taught that conquerors were well-meaning politicians who made the world a better place, not bloodletting psychopaths who were bent on conquest and the eradication of inferior races a la Adolf Hitler.

For these successful campaigns, violent exterminations, and purge of political opponents, the Senate

This likeness of Octavian is embossed on the obverse of a contemporary Roman coin that is dated 12 B.C. on the reverse. (I am only kidding about the date.) Photo from the author's collection.

awarded him the honorary title of Augustus, meaning "illustrious one." Octavian's formal name and title became Gaius Julius Caesar Augustus. He was then the Imperator, or Emperor, of Rome. The history books mostly forego his misdeeds and dwell on his accomplishments as the absolute ruler of Pax Romana (Roman Peace) when he embarked upon more peaceful goals such as building temples, patronizing the arts, encouraging agriculture, and maintaining the economy (by means of slavery of the masses, also left out of the history books).

Note that I have Octavian to thank as a patron of the arts for enabling Vergil to write the *Aeneid* (the Latin version of the Greek poet Homer's *Iliad* and *Odyssey*), which I had to read in its original language during my fourth year of Latin as a senior in high school. The ongoing joke in class was that the greatest accomplishment of the Romans was that they understood Latin. I hope they understood it better than I did.

Also note that Octavian was emperor of Rome at the time of the birth of Jesus Christ, but died before the crucifixion and martyrdom of the Savior.

It is to be hoped that the *Octavian* was named after the eponymous emperor's constructive endeavors, as opposed to his means for achieving those endeavors. Keep in mind that every conqueror throughout history can also be described as an egomaniac, a terrorist, a mass murderer, an executioner, a torturer, and so on. Octavian is a prime example.

Octavian (in italics, meaning the vessel)

In 1938, the *Octavian* departed on her maiden voyage as a tramp freighter. A tramp freighter is one which does not maintain scheduled voyages between the same two ports, but is directed to collect cargo at one port and deliver it to another, after which it is directed to a third port to collect cargo and deliver it to yet another. In other words, it tramps around the world in order to collect cargoes of opportunity, and to deliver those cargoes to their arranged destinations, wherever they may be. Such a freighter may not return to its home port for months or even years.

It was fortunate for the *Octavian* that she was not in her home port of Bergen on April 9, 1940. That was the day on which Nazi military forces launched a surprise attack on Norway. If the Nazis expected an uncontested invasion, they were sadly mistaken, for they were met with fierce resistance from local military forces. For two months the Norwegian army and navy fought against overwhelming odds. They were supported by British troops until Germany invaded France, on May 10, 1940. When the British diverted some of its support of Norway in order to help France beat back the Nazis on the French eastern front, the Nazis took advantage of the weaker Norwegian military.

Fighting in Norway continued for another month, but by early June the Norwegian armed forces were no longer able to defend their positions. Norway capitulated on June 10, 1940. The Norwegian government, including the royal family, managed to escape from the country by air before occupational forces were firmly established. They spent the remainder of the war in exile as guests of Great Britain and the United States.

The dreaded swastika flew above Norway for the next five years.

Swastika

The swastika has a long and fascinating history. The design can be traced back as far as 10,000 years. Its first known appearance was carved onto a mammoth tusk that was found in the Ukraine. A more stylistic form of the swastika was found cut into stone in a British moor. A Bulgarian cave yielded pottery that was adorned with a pair of facing swastikas: one clockwise and the other counterclockwise; the ceramic material was dated to be some 8,000 years old. The device was found on an Indian seal that is thought to be more than 5,000 years old. A 3,000-year-old necklace with attached brooches was unearthed in Iran.

Below left: This early 20th-century medallion symbolized the way good luck charms were pictured in a number of ancient and modern cultures, with the swastika being predominant. Below right: Author Rudyard Kipling had the swastika embossed on his books as a way to patronize the good luck for which it stood.

This postcard was a popular style in the 1920's, when the swastika was equivalent to the four-leafed clover with regard to luck and good fortune . . . before Hitler made the swastika a symbol of horrification.

In short, representations of the swastika have been found in many forms wherever early mankind has inhabited the land. This includes Bronze Age and Iron Age cultures in Europe, Russia, India, China, and Africa.

As civilization evolved and became more complex, the swastika was often used with other stylistic line combinations, as an artistic design without particular meaning or connotation. For example, the swastika adorned coins in Mesopotamia.

Gradually, the swastika was assimilated into ancient religions where it assumed spiritual significance. Forever afterward, the swastika was in some way symbolic, with various meanings that had nothing to do with the shape of the symbol.

In its simplest form, the swastika adorned doorways the way horseshoes are employed in western homes: to bring luck or health to those who pass under the lintel. Religious beliefs and rites differ in accordance with the dogmas of the believers; the swastika could represent continuity or encircling, such as the (apparent) revolving sun or ongoing creation or infinity. Once the swastika became an object of reverence, the ways in which it was interpreted grew in accordance with the spread of cults and theological sects.

The swastika was charmed with endless symbolisms. For thousands of years, in countries the world over, the most important feature of the swastika's symbolic meaning was positive. Even unto the first third of the twentieth century, the swastika always represented some facet of goodness or happiness. . . .

. . . . until Adolf Hitler chose the swastika to represent the Nazi party.

Forever more, the swastika must remain a symbol of Aryan aggression, of war, of gross destruction, of global terrorism, of torture, of mass executions, all in the name of world domination.

Nazi Occupation

German occupation meant that all vessels that were docked in Norwegian ports at the time of Norway's surrender were confiscated by the Nazi regime. Because the *Octavian* was at sea at the time of the invasion, and remained out of the country during the subsequent conflict, she was able to continue her career as a Norwegian freighter that operated under Allied command. Her Norwegian crew remained on board as expatriates: tramping the seven seas while her Norwegian owners operated in exile from offices in Great Britain. In this manner the *Octavian* and her merchant mariners served and fought against the Nazis.

The obvious corollary to this situation meant that Norwegian sailors could not return home in order to visit with their families and friends. Those Norwegian sailors who were separated from their wives and children were forced to remain separated for the duration of the war. By the same token, wives and children, and mothers and fathers, often had no news of their husbands, fathers, and sons: whether they were safe and healthy, or even if they were still alive. This hardship put a strain on everyone at sea as well as at home.

The sad fate of Norwegian sailors who were killed in action was unknown by their families at home until the end of Nazi occupation. Norway was occupied for five years: from April 9, 1940 to May 8, 1945.

Norwegian sailors rose through the ranks from lowly positions such as mess boys or galley boys or deck boys. These "boys" were young teenagers under the age of 18 years: young men who in today's world would be considered children who had not yet graduated from high school. The youngest "boy" on record was only 14 years of age when he was killed in action: a true boy by anyone's estimation. Many other boys were among the dead and missing when their ship was sunk beneath them by a Nazi U-boat. Those who survived and attained their education at sea became experienced seamen, machinists, even officers.

The oldest Norwegian seaman to die at sea as a result of Hitler's bid for world domination was 67 years of age. No matter the number of years that a seaman spent on Earth, every fatality was a personal tragedy.

Hundreds of Norwegians were captured at sea and spent the rest of the war in German, Japanese, or French concentration camps. Many Norwegian seamen perished in captivity as a result of malnutrition and mistreatment. Those who survived the Axis death camps required a long time for rehabilitation. Some never recovered completely.

Thousands of Norwegian seamen did not return home after the cessation of hos-

This 1936 German postage stamp represented the turning point in the meaning of the swastika. The raised hands show the "Heil Hitler" salute, or Seig Heil (Hail Victory), which displayed obedience to the Nazi Party.

tilities. Their bodies were never found. They simply vanished at sea, either at the time their ships were sunk, or later after perishing in lifeboats from thirst, starvation, or exposure to the elements of nature: a painful and lingering death whose suffering is ineffable.

In addition, nearly a thousand seamen who were citizens of other nations died on Norwegian ships during the war. Hitler truly touched them all: with the warhead of a torpedo, the shell of a deck gun, or a bullet from a machine gun.

Despite their patriotism under fire, Norwegian sailors were badly treated by their fellow citizens when they eventually returned home at the end of the war. They were viewed not as heroes who kept fighting the Nazis by manning ships that transported food and materiel in support of the Allied war effort. They were branded mostly as deserters – as if they had anything to say or do about their enforced absence from home.

Sadly, this reminds me of my own experiences after being sent home from Vietnam, in a body cast. I can't count the number of times that people cursed at me, spit on me, or called me dirty names, with "baby killer" being the most prevalent epithet. I didn't ask to go to Vietnam. My government gave me a choice of two years in the Army or five years in a federal penitentiary. I made the wrong choice, and I've been suffering for it for my entire adult life. It seems that American citizens were as bad in the 1960's and 1970's as Norwegian citizens were in the 1940's. Some human nature never changes.

Tramping the World

During her short career of just over three years, the *Octavian* operated as a tramp freighter. As already noted, in maritime circles, "tramp" is not a derogatory word. It does not recall depression-era hoboes hitching rides on railroad freight cars. According to *The Nautical Cyclopedia* (1995), by this author, a tramp freighter is "a freighter which does not have a scheduled route between specific ports, but which picks up a cargo wherever it may be and transports it to its consigned destination, from which the freighter will pick up another cargo and take it to *its* destination. Thus the ship 'tramps' around the world, and may not return to its home port for years."

As an example, take the final four months of the *Octavian's* voyages. She departed from Pensacola, Florida on September 20, and arrived at Mobile, Alabama on the same day. She departed from Mobile on September 24, and arrived at Galveston, Texas on September 26. She departed from Galveston on September 27, and arrived at Port Alfred, Quebec on October 10. She departed from Port Alfred on October 11, and arrived at Montreal, Quebec on October 12. She departed from Montreal on October 16, and arrived at St. John's, Newfoundland on October 20. She departed from St. John's on October 26, and arrived at Botwood, Newfoundland on October 28. She departed from Botwood on November 1, and arrived at Beaumont, Texas on November 18.

Subsequent voyages took the *Octavian* to Port Arthur, Texas; Galveston, Texas; St. John, New Brunswick; Botwood, Quebec; on January 4, 1942 she steamed to Pensacola, Florida, thence to New Orleans, Louisiana, thence to Galveston, thence to . . . She was headed for St. John, New Brunswick, but never reached her destination. Her itinerary ends with "OVERDUE presumed lost between 16/1 – 19/1/42." (Note that Norwegian date protocol gives the day before the month instead of the month before the day.)

The *Octavian's* cargo on her final voyage was 1,345 tons of sulfur in the form of crystalline mineral rock. In ancient times, sulfur was known as brimstone. Nowadays, the word brimstone is generally used only in the phrase "fire and brimstone," which signifies the wrath of the Christian God.

High school students should be familiar with sulfur. Whenever the chemistry lab burned hydrogen sulfide, the odor of rotten eggs permeated the building.

Sulfur (which used to be spelled sulphur, whose chemical symbol is S) has numerous uses. In a variety of chemical compounds, sulfur is a crucial element that facilitates biochemical processes in living animals. Because sulfur is prevalent in so many plant and animal organisms, it is consumed naturally without the need for artificial supplements. In industry, the greatest uses of sulfur are in fixing man-made fertilizers and producing sulfuric acid.

More important than the loss of a modern and valuable ship, plus 1,345 tons of raw sulfur, was the demise of the *Octavian's* crew. These seventeen men were:

Jens L. Dahl, Captain
Herman Bertinsen, First Mate
Olaf N. Nilsen, Second Mate
Sigurd Fosse, First Engineer
Johan Rashback Egholm,
    Second Engineer
Haakon Mjelde, Third Engineer
Robert N. Thomsen, Donkeyman
Peder Berntsen, Stoker
Olaf Brudvik, Stoker
Suren Johan Mousen, Stoker
Ole Peder Olsen, Steward
Konrad Skarshaug, Cook
Edvard Dahle, Able Seaman
Lars Eftang Olsen, Able Seaman
Erling Ostby, Ordinary Seaman
Alf Aune Pedersen, Ordinary Seaman
Albert Leonard Pott (Canadian), Ordinary Seaman

This chunk of sulfur measures 3.5 inches by 2.75 inches.

A different list claims that there were eighteen men on the *Octavian* at the time of her loss. The additional man was given as Lars Lothe, Second Mate.

Thus ended the *Octavian*, her cargo, and her crew. May they rest in peace forever.

C2 - In Pursuit of Shipwrecks

In the early days of wreck-diving, discovering shipwrecks was a haphazard affair that did not occur very often. The reason was that charter boat skippers did not want to waste diesel fuel or gasoline to plow the open ocean for something that they did not care about. They could make more money simply by taking divers to known wreck sites, then returning to the dock and collecting charter fees.

This attitude was not as harsh as it sounds. The vast majority of divers did not care about which wreck they visited, as long as it was loaded with lobsters they could catch, fish they could spear, or shellfish they could collect. They were not wreck-divers: that is, divers who wanted to find and/or explore shipwrecks. They were food divers. Because most of the shallow water wrecks had long since been found – usually by head boats – food divers had a multitude of places to dive. One more was neither here nor there; or if they were, they were not worth searching for when a sure thing was close at hand and ripe for the harvest.

Among early ocean diving enthusiasts there existed a small coterie of divers who were more interested in the exploration value of a wreck than the foodstuff that it might yield. These divers were in the minority, so there was no need to cater to their needs. As a result, few to no charter boat skippers were actively searching for unfound shipwrecks.

This situation started to change in the 1990's. It was no coincidence that this was also the time of the proliferation of technical diving. Divers who wanted to challenge themselves by diving deeper needed deeper wrecks to dive on. Thus entered the era of offshore wreck diving.

Recreational diving commenced a downward spiral at the turn of the twenty-first century. This was due almost entirely to nationwide economic woes: an issue that accelerated drastically with the housing market crash in the summer of 2008. Fewer divers signed up for scuba training courses. Many dive shops went out of business. Dedicated dive charter boats turned to fishing as their primary source of income. Many boats ceased to operate. Technical diving all but vanished.

Those technical divers who wanted to continue diving deep, needed another way to reach deep shipwrecks. Now entered a new era: this one of privately owned dive boats. In this regimen, boat owners could dive whenever they wanted, and wherever they wanted. Furthermore, they were not restricted to destinations that were chosen by charter boat skippers, so they could search for unfound shipwrecks.

This fad was not terribly new. In the 1970's, a group of New York City divers who called themselves the Aquarians owned their own boat. Each club member was part owner who shared expenses and responsibilities. At that time they were unique.

In the late 1990's and early 2000's, with the number of commercial dive boats shrinking, several New York and New Jersey individuals

The *Aquarian II* was a bigger and badder version of the original *Aquarian*.

either took the same route or catered to divers who wanted to search for virgin wrecks, of which I can name a few (in alphabetical order): Bob Archambault (*Robin II*), Dan Bartone (*Independence II*), Dan Crowell (*Seeker*), Joe Mazraani (*Tenacious*), and Bob Meimbreese (*Down Deep*). These boat owners started as divers, then obtained a boat in order to have more freedom to select diving destinations.

These skippers all carried Coast Guard certifications and licenses.

Others, who are more pertinent to the story at hand, were Rusty Cassway and Brian Sullivan (*Explorer*), Harold Moyers (*Big Mac*), and Sean Manni (*Jersey Dragon*). All of them were skilled technical divers who actively searched for unfound shipwrecks.

Keep in mind that searching for shipwrecks offers no guarantee of finding them. More often than not, either no wrecks are found; or if a wreck is found, it turns out to be an old wooden barge or a recent trawler or dragger, neither of which have much historical value.

Robin II

Bob Archambault was a mainstay in the diving industry. In the 1970's, he belonged to the Eastern Divers Association: a group of deep decompression divers who initiated a policy of shipwreck exploration. EDA was organized by Elliot Subervi, then headed by Tom Roach when Elliot handed him the reins. Bob later bought a boat that had sufficient range to go offshore where most other dive boats couldn't reach.

Gene Peterson possessed some offshore hang numbers that had strong possibilities of being undived wreck sites. They were located some sixty miles at sea, in the area where I had placed the six unfortunate vessels that were known as the Black Sunday Wrecks, all of which had been sunk by the Kaiser's U-boat *U-151* (Korvettenkapitan Heinrich von Nostitz) on June 2, 1918.

Gene chartered the boat for a three-day trip, then obtained a group of divers who were capable of diving to 200 feet and deeper. In addition to Gene, onboard were Steve Gatto, Peter Hess, Ken Mason, John Moyer, Tom Packer, John Yurga, and this author.

On July 25, 1995, we discovered the wreck of an old steamship that lay at a depth of 220 feet. I recovered a porthole that was stamped "GEBRS. KRAMER ROTTERDAM." Other divers rescued china plates with the monogram "HAL," which stood for Hamburg American Line.

I didn't know what this portended at the moment, but at home I searched through my files for vessels that were lost in the vicinity, especially the Black Sunday wrecks. I hit pay dirt right away. The Dutch freighter *Texel* was built in Rotterdam, the Netherlands. The length of the wreck agreed with the *Texel's* length of 331 feet. The layout of the superstructure matched as well. On a subsequent trip I found five brass letters that spelled the vessel's name on the bow.

Independence II

I was fortunate enough to share some of Dan Bartone's experiences in searching for shipwrecks. The one that I remember most fondly was the day that Frankie Pellegrino showed up at the dock with a side-scan sonar unit, both towfish and console.

Frankie was a New York City policeman whose primary occupation on the force was working with the Big Apple's underwater search and recovery team. For a living he commonly dived in the City's creeks and rivers in search of dead bodies and criminal evidence. Lest this sound like a dream job come true, understand that visibility in the water seldom exceeded that of zero feet, where the viz was measured in finger widths, like whiskey. He was more likely to find a Long Island whitefish (a used condom) floating in mid-water than the object of his search.

These perquisites of the job notwithstanding, he did manage to borrow the brand-new and never used sonar fish for calibration experiments. Because heavy weather precluded diving for the day, we repaired to a local picnic ground where interference was lacking. According to the instructions, we had to stretch the cables between the transmitter and receiver in an area that was far away from metal that would distort the signal. The grassy lawn was perfect for the occasion.

Frankie uncrated the unit from the heavy wooden box. The fish measured some five feet in length, and looked very much like a 1950's version of a planetary spaceship, complete with four vanes near the tail for stabilization.

Always quick with a quip, I said, "Whatever you do, do not put this thing on your shoulder and point it at any tall buildings." (This was shortly after the terrorist attack on the Twin Towers.)

Within minutes, a patrol car stopped nearby, and a police officer casually walked over to ask what we were doing. Frankie identified himself, explained the situation, showed him the tow fish, and exhibited the operating manual. The cop was satisfied, and quickly returned to more important business such as issuing speeding tickets to motorists. This commercial approach to police work was more rewarding than catching criminals because, as everyone knows, crime doesn't pay.

Seeker

Bill Nagle was the first owner of the *Seeker*. He purchased the stagnating boat from the builder because the person who had ordered it had died before construction was completed. Bill named her the *Seeker* because of his avowed intention to seek undiscovered shipwrecks, and to more fully explore shipwrecks that had been neglected. To describe two examples:

First, he organized an overnight trip to the armored cruiser *San Diego*, and furnished an underwater suction device with which to remove sand from the admiral's and captain's quarters, thus uncovering and then recovering artifacts that would today be buried under tons of steel after the upside-down hull collapsed.

Second, he organized a five-day trip to the Italian liner *Andrea Doria* in order to search for and recover the ship's bell. This mission met with setbacks in the search but ultimately ended successfully. The bell has since been displayed at numerous public venues.

Somewhere along the way Bill lost his purpose, and instead started a commercial charter business. He did very little seeking after that.

One of his greatest claims to fame – and well deserved – occurred in 1988 when, on the return from an offshore charter, he checked a set of coordinates that he had obtained from the Bogans: a commercial fishing family that had been in business since the 1930's. After two previous deep dives, none of the divers had sufficient surface interval to explore the wreck, but two divers volunteered to make a bounce dive in order to confirm the existence of a shipwreck instead of the strong possibility that the spike on the depth recorder marked a reef or rock pile.

Those two divers were Chuck Wine and Bart Malone. Bart experienced narcosis on the way down the anchor line, and did not reach the bottom. Chuck went all the way to the seabed, which lay at a depth of 230 feet. He was astonished to see that the grapnel was hooked into the wreckage of a long tubular hull that was narrow and rounded. There was no doubt in his mind that he was looking at a submarine, and he said so to Bill after he returned to the boat.

Bill did not return to the site until three years later, at which time every diver confirmed Chuck's description. The submarine was later identified as the *U-869*, about which two books have been written:

Shadow Divers (2004) and *Shadow Divers Exposed* (2006). The first book was a fictional account that was overwritten and grossly embellished with impossible factoids. The second book was my refutation, filled with proofs that repudiated the fabricated stories with which the first book was riddled: proofs that were supported by documentation and interviews with the actual participants.

After Bill's untimely demise, Dan Crowell bought the *Seeker* as a commercial venture that would not only show a profit, but would also enable him to dive on the wrecks to which he was taking his paying customers. Having said (or written) that, I should add that Crowell was a hard-core wreck-diver himself, and one who took the advantage of owning his own boat to run captain's charters in order to search for offshore shipwrecks, most of which were deep enough to be categorized as technical dives, perhaps requiring breathing gases that included helium. The captain's charters were organized by invitation only, and the divers who signed up for those trips were his friends or divers whose qualifications were well-known to him.

In his heyday, Dan also ran annual trips to the *Andrea Doria.*

The discovery that concerns us here is the *Pan-Pennsylvania.* Due to the distance from the *Seeker's* dock in Brielle, New Jersey, we spent three days and two nights at sea. The goal of the trip was to check a location that we hoped was the site of the *U-550.* On the way to the target, we checked another set of numbers that proved to be a wreck of substantial size. We did not dive on it but proceeded as planned.

We spent several hours in criss-crossing the area around the coordinates that purposed to be U-boat wreck site, but found nothing on the depth sounder other than a flat and featureless bottom. Even broadening the area brought no worthwhile results. After admitting defeat, we moved to another set of numbers that was supposed to be the site of the *Pan-Pennsylvania*: the tanker that the *U-550* torpedoed before it was depth-charged and sunk by a bevy of escort vessels. What follows is the story of both actions.

Official U.S. Coast Guard photo.

Generally, when a vessel is fitted with two or more engines, each engine turns its own shaft and propeller. The machinery of the *Pan-Pennsylvania* was interesting in that both steam turbines were geared to a single shaft. The engines were built by the Allis-Chalmers Manufacturing Company, in Milwaukee, Wisconsin. The propulsion machinery was located aft. The hull plates were arc welded electrically. Her gross registered tonnage was 11,017.

Because the tanker was constructed during the war, she was armed with two deck guns for protection against German U-boats. A 3-inch gun was mounted forward; a 4-inch gun was mounted aft. As the tanker's intended purpose was to deliver cargoes to England and the European theater, where German aircraft abounded, 20-millimeter anti-aircraft guns were mounted in tubs atop the midship wheelhouse, atop the after structure between the deck gun and the smokestack, and on elevated platforms between the wheelhouse and the after structure. For full coverage at each location, these anti-aircraft guns were emplaced along both sides, with half the barrels trained to port and half trained to starboard. Shrapnel shields protected all guns and gunners.

In addition to four lifeboats, four emergency life rafts were secured to side-mounted racks for immediate deployment.

The *Pan-Pennsylvania* departed from New York on April 15, 1944, bound for the United Kingdom in Convoy CU-21, which consisted of twenty-eight merchant vessels and six armed escorts. She carried 140,000 barrels of 80-octane gasoline in her cargo tanks. She also carried seven airplanes and seven boxes topside. On board were eighty-one men: fifty officers and crewmembers, and thirty-one armed guards whose responsibility it was to man the guns.

The convoy got off to a slow start because of fog that shrouded New York Harbor. Only with difficulty did the vessels navigate safely through the swept channel (that part of the shipping channel that was swept clear of mines, and whose sides were marked by buoys that delineated the safe travel zone from the friendly minefields that guarded the outer perimeter). Instead of proceeding southeast along the Mud Hole to the Hudson Canyon, as originally intended, the convoy turned due east in

Note the dearth of marine life on the *Pan-Pennsylvania*.

order to avoid an inbound convoy. The sun set before the merchant vessels in the convoy could be notified of the change. Darkness and fog precluded blinker communication, so the escorts felt their way through the mist-laden blackness and notified each vessel individually of the diversion. This action was necessitated by radio blackout.

While maneuvering through the darkness and fog, in order to comply with the change of plan, fate conspired to bring two ships together with a crunch of steel on steel. The Honduran freighter *Aztec* collided with the U.S. tanker *Sag Harbor*. Neither vessel was in danger of sinking, but both were in need of repairs. The destroyer escort *Peterson* was ordered to escort the damaged vessels back to port.

After this auspicious beginning, the convoy increased its speed to

14 knots. The merchant vessels proceeded in two roughly parallel columns, while the five remaining escort vessels swept the outboard sides with their radar and sonar units. All went well until 8 o'clock in the morning, about 150 miles east of Ambrose light. By that time the fog had dissipated to a slight haze. The wind was moderate from the north-northeast, and the seas were running in slight swells. The convoy had gotten somewhat disjointed in the limited visibility, so the merchant vessels were jockeying for position in order to reform into columns. After seeing her charges safely to harbor, the *Peterson* raced at 30 knots in order to rejoin the convoy.

On the *Pan-Pennsylvania*, nine lookouts were maintaining a sharp watch: two crewmembers on the port and starboard wings of the bridge, and seven armed guards – two forward, one on the flying bridge, two amidship, and two aft. Other vessels of the convoy were in sight.

By 1944, the heyday of U-boat successes was far in the past. Aggressive U-boat commanders often found themselves the hunted instead of the hunter. The first U-boats to desecrate American waters found the shipping lanes largely unprotected, and merchant vessels proceeding independently: prime targets that were sometimes silhouetted against lights on shore. German sailors referred to those days as the Happy Times, or the Great American Turkey Shoot. In the Eastern Sea Frontier – which extended from Canada to the Georgia-Florida border – the first six months of 1942 saw the loss of more than 120 vessels and the death of more than 2,500 men, women, and children.

Now the tables were turned. Attacks in waters that were protected by U.S. Navy warships were more like suicide missions than enemy patrols. Every U-boat that was bold enough – or stupid enough – to fire torpedoes into an escorted convoy found itself mercilessly trounced by depth charges and hedgehogs, and surrounded by escorts that clung to sonar traces like terriers worrying rats. Few U-boats escaped, and those that did usually slunk away severely damaged.

Kapitanleutnant Klaus Hanert, captain of the *U-550*, cannot be accused of pusillanimity. He chanced upon convoy CU-21 while it was reforming after its twenty-eight merchant vessels had been dispersed in the nighttime fog. Dawn found six armed escorts herding their wayward charges together like sheep dogs tending their flock. Slowly the convoy was reorganized into twin columns.

The six destroyer escorts were the *Gandy, Harveson, Joyce, Kirkpatrick, Peterson,* and *Poole.* Three escorts prowled outboard of each side of the convoy, sweeping the sea ahead of them with finely tuned sonar units. Highly trained sound operators sat with headsets over their ears, listening intently. Yet none detected the U-boat before its torpedo struck the *Pan-Pennsylvania* at 8:05 in the morning of April 16, 1944.

Without warning, the torpedo struck the port side of the *Pan-Pennsylvania* at #8 tank. The tank exploded with a deafening concussion that heaved and cracked the deck. "Steam line to blower broken, steering gear went out although telemotor could have been used and communication was gone." Number four lifeboat disappeared in the blast. The engine room bilges flooded immediately with seawater. Shortly thereafter, the inrush of gasoline from the ruptured tank compartment set the engine room afire.

The tanker was sorely struck and was in danger of sinking.

Captain Delmar Leidy, master, ordered the engines reversed and the tanker turned hard to port. He did *not* give the order to abandon ship. Nonetheless, several crewmembers and armed guards panicked – they were perched above eight tanks of high-octane gasoline whose volatile and explosive nature was an established fact – and started to lower the surviving lifeboats. Number three hit the water while considerable way was still on the ship. The lifeboat capsized and dumped its occupants into the water, where they drowned. Several others leaped from the tall deck of the tanker; they, too, were lost.

Captain Leidy struggled to restore order. The forward gun crew fired a shell from the 3-inch gun, despite the fact that no target was in sight. A guardsman on #4 anti-aircraft gun was injured "by explosion."

The *Pan-Pennsylvania* was settling slowly by the stern. A growing pool of gasoline surrounded the hull. The danger of sinking was not imminent, but the danger that the floating gasoline might catch fire was a distinct probability, especially in light of the fact that the engine room and boiler room were still engulfed in flames. After the tanker came to a halt, the captain ordered the launching of the two remaining lifeboats. The holding chocks were knocked off the life raft racks so that the rafts could be tipped overboard, or could float free when the vessel sank. "Confidential orders were all thrown overboard except Mersig Vol. I, Zigzag and Convoy Orders, which were last seen in the chart room."

USS *Peterson* (DE 152)   Courtesy of the Naval Photographic Center.

At this point the ship was abandoned in a nearly orderly fashion. Anxiety created haste in the lowering of lifeboat #2, on the weather side, as a result of which three men were crushed between the lifeboat and the hull. Of the total complement, 56 men were accounted for and 25 men were missing (15 crewmembers and 10 armed guards). One body was recovered.

The three destroyer escorts that were patrolling the tanker's side of the convoy were the *Gandy*, *Joyce*, and *Peterson*. They detached themselves from the convoy. The *Joyce* proceeded to search for survivors while the *Peterson* provided cover.

As the men sat in their boats awaiting rescue, *Gandy* conducted a radar sweep by steaming in an arc at flank speed. She was wise to take precautions, for a torpedo raced past her on a parallel course, missing the warship by seventy-five yards. The *Gandy* took immediate aggressive action by turning and speeding along the torpedo's track toward its point of origination. She failed to establish sonar contact. Worse, overheated cylinders cracked the crankcase of number four engine, forcing her to reduce her speed.

Despite the imbalance that resulted from proceeding without one engine, the *Gandy* continued to sweep the seas with her sonar as she returned to the scene of the catastrophe. By now the *Pan-Pennsylvania* was settling rapidly by the stern. The survivors found themselves in dire straits. The tanker was surrounded by a growing pool of gasoline, the ignition of which was threatened by a fire in the engine room.

The *Joyce* was overwhelmed by her rescue efforts, so the *Peterson* hove to in order to lend assistance. The *Gandy* circled the sitting ducks in order to provide protection.

Another torpedo track passed close aboard the *Gandy*. By observing the direction of the track, her officers determined that the wily U-boat was hiding under and close alongside the sinking tanker, effectively masking it from sonar detection.

By this time the *Joyce* had rescued the last of the survivors. She raced toward a target which her astute sound operator heard through his headphones. She dropped a pattern of thirteen depth charges that were set to detonate after a shallow descent. The bow of the U-boat was blown to the surface by the force of the underwater explosions.

On the bridge of the crippled *Gandy*, Lieutenant Commander W.A. Sessions shouted, "Right full rudder, come to 320, open fire, and stand by to ram!" The U-boat's forward momentum was more than Commander Sessions calculated. He quickly ordered the rudder thrown back to port. With collision imminent, Lieutenant H.W. Perkerson ordered the hoisting of the sound head.

Note: At this point I must bifurcate my narrative. On one hand I have information from the American action reports; on the other hand I have interviews with two rescued German sailors. Joe Mazraani interviewed these two German sailors in 2012, after he discovered the wreck of the U-550 (which see below). I make no comment about the difference in the narratives.

Action report: Unable to submerge, German sailors poured out of

The *U-550* surfacing in the foreground as the *Pan-Pennsylvania* burns in the background. (Courtesy of the National Archives.)

the conning tower hatch. The Americans on the destroyer escorts presumed that the Germans intended to man the anti-aircraft guns. Commander Sessions aimed his ship at the U-boat's after gun mount. The *Gandy* missed the intended target by twenty-five feet. The bow of the destroyer escort scraped across the hull of the U-boat immediately abaft the deadly armament. The *Gandy*'s rudder was kept at "full left" in order to throw the propellers clear. Accompanying the awful grinding scrape of steel on steel was the cacophony of gunfire that was directed at the U-boat.

The *Gandy* and the U-boat ran along a parallel course. Guns from the destroyer escort continued to rake the conning tower and gun positions of the U-boat, until Commander Sessions heard a voice "on one of our voice radios shouting something in a Germanic accent. Supposing it an offer to surrender, I ordered 'cease firing' which, after a few seconds delay, got through to the guns. Almost immediately the sub manned a machine gun battery and commenced firing on us. We swung left to bring guns to bear."

The deck of the U-boat was littered with the dead and dying. Aboard the *Gandy*, four men lay wounded as a result of overlapping and ricocheting friendly fire from the surrounding destroyer escorts.

Interview: No German sailors were on the deck of the U-boat. No one manned the anti-aircraft guns. The German sailors only wanted to escape the sinking U-boat.

Action report: Tracer rounds from the running gun battle between the U-boat and the destroyer escorts glanced off the tanker's hull, and ignited the surrounding pool of gasoline. The sea suddenly erupted in flames that engulfed the abandoned tanker. Slowly, almost languorously, the *Pan-Pennsylvania* settled and rolled over until she lay upside down with her stern on the bottom – and there she hung.

The *Peterson* cornered the surfaced U-boat from the other side of the *Gandy*, and fired two shallow-set depth charges from her starboard K-guns (depth-charge launchers). Severely holed and damaged, the U-boat became unmanageable. Kapitanleutnant Klaus Hanert gave two orders: set scuttling charges and abandon ship. An explosion ripped open the pressure hull aft. The U-boat sank by the stern, leaving only thirteen crewmembers to be rescued. The *Joyce* picked up the survivors.

Interview: Three men climbed from the control room to the conning tower: the captain, the battle helmsman, and the boatswain. Their intention was not to man the machine gun, but to fire a torpedo. All three were shot by marine gun fire from the destroyer escorts. Hanert was wounded and fell through the hatch into the control room. The other two were killed as bullets shredded the conning tower casing. From the control room, someone fired a flair through the hatch without climbing up the ladder. Only after the shelling stopped did anyone escape from the pressure hull.

Action report: The *Gandy* suffered the loss of four feet of her reinforced bow strake. Several antennas were shot away, and her hull was punctured with numerous .50 caliber holes. For a warship only eight days out of shakedown, her crew had performed their duties extraordinarily well under their baptism of fire.

One of the U-boat's survivors died of his injuries, and was buried at sea the following day. The remaining twelve, including Hanert, were imprisoned aboard the *Joyce*. All three escort vessels rejoined the convoy and completed the transatlantic crossing. The German prisoners were turned over to authorities in Londonderry, Northern Ireland. The survivors of the *Pan-Pennsylvania* were also disembarked.

On May 5, fully nineteen days after the double tragedy, the Coastal Picket Patrol Boat *CGR-3082* came across a body at sea: that of a German sailor wearing an escape lung. An autopsy report indicated no injuries other than burns on the head and face, probably from diesel oil; that the sailor had died prior to submersion, as though he had been on a raft; and that he had died only five days previous. The conclusion was that he had escaped from the sunken *U-550* from where it lay on the seabed, and died on the surface.

Two other bodies were later found in the vicinity of the sunken U-boat. The body picked up by the *SC-630* had been in the water for more than eighteen days. The body recovered by the *CGR-1989* on May 11 was not only wearing an escape lung and life vest, but was sitting in a rubber raft; he was Wilhelm Flade, last of the *U-550's* casualties to be found.

Interview: No one was left aboard the U-boat. All had escaped from the pressure hull and jumped into the sea.

Action report: The *Pan-Pennsylvania* did not sink on the day of the attack (April 16). Her bow protruded precariously above the surface, a clear hazard to navigation. The next day, a bevy of Navy vessels were dispatched to the site in the hope that the vessel could be salvaged. The depth of water – 250 feet – made total hull salvage impossible. Instead, the USS *Sagamore* (which was designated as the vessel in command) directed that the *General Greene*, *Harriet Lane*, *Hazel*, and *Rescue* "line up in formation and fire into hull of tanker to try to sink her. After several turns at firing at hull and dropping depth charges, tanker still remained afloat and continued burning." The *Sagamore* "directed all vessels to cease firing and standby."

They stood by all night. At noon on April 18, a flight of bombers arrived at the scene to complete the task of destruction. These planes finally bombed the *Pan-Pennsylvania* into submersion.

On April 20, the *General Greene* and *Harriet Lane* deployed two "Dan" buoys near the sunken tanker: one 500 yards north of the wreck, and one 500 yards south of the wreck. Then they dropped a fifty-pound grapple and "dragged area determining wreck to be on bottom." Next they deployed a 600-pound spherical buoy with a two-ton mooring.

On April 21, the *General Greene* recovered the "Dan" buoys. She then proceeded to the Nantucket Shoal Whistle Buoy in order to determine the "distance and bearing of wreck from this aid to navigation. Wreck of *Pan Pennsylvania* lies 14.1 miles 196° T[rue] of buoy #468." Attempts to recover the spherical buoy proved unsuccessful due to rough seas.

Initially, the latitude and longitude were recorded as 40° 7' north, 69° 30' west. This was later corrected to 40-23-20 north, 69-36-30 west. The location of the sunken tanker was plotted on navigational charts with a wreck symbol. The site has long been known to commercial anglers, but never identified by wreck-divers.

The wreck was first dived on July 9, 1994. Those who dived on the wreck that discovery day were John Chatterton, Ken Clayton, Dan Crowell, Tom Hirose, Barb Lander, Brad Sheard, Brian Skerry, Harvey Storck, and this author.

German sailors crowd the wintergarden of the *U-550*, not to man the deck gun but to surrender and plead for rescue from the sinking U-boat. (Courtesy of the National Archives.)

We were sadly disappointed at the condition of the wreck. We expected such a large vessel to rise high off the bottom and to possess a considerable amount of complex structure to explore. Instead, we found that most of the upside-down wreck had settled into the sand. The entire superstructure was buried. Only the lower hull was exposed.

The depth of the seabed was 250 feet. The maximum relief was twenty feet. The flat bottom was topped by a pair of bilge keels that were separated by a distance of about 30 feet. From the high side – outboard of the bilge keels – one can slide down the vertical portion of the outer hull to the seabed. Very little of the hull has collapsed, so that debris fields are practically nonexistent. Fish traps were in evidence, as were segments of nets. Visibility was ten to fifteen feet.

The dive was one that I would describe as "blah." Because the wreck lay upside down, I saw nothing but the bottom steel plates of the hull. I looked through a few rust holes, but saw only the inner plates of the double hull. Everyone else concurred that the wreck was not worth a second dive.

Before I segue into the next section I would like to insert an interlude. We all voted to take a chance on diving on the wreck that we had marked on the outward passage. Chatterton dived first and tied in the grapnel. After he released a Styrofoam cup, whose appearance on the surface meant that the anchor line was secure, I was the next one in the water. During my exploration to a depth of 250 feet, I found the ship's bell, on which was etched the name of the wreck: *Sebastian.*

After my return home with the bell safely in hand, I went through my shipwreck files and found that I had annotated the wreck some twenty years previous, but marked it too deep to dive! Such was the state of recreational diving before the inception of technical diving.

The *Sebastian* was a 310-foot-long British tanker that sank in 1917 after catching fire when ready fuel oil overflowed accidentally and came in contact with the exhaust piping of one of the main engines.

I wrote a magazine article about the *Sebastian's* discovery and history, ending with a morality lesson about the difference between being first and being observant: "The early bird gets the worm, but the second mouse gets the cheese."

Tenacious

Joe Mazraani bought the *Tenacious* for the primary purpose of using her to locate the long-sought German U-boat *U-550.* As noted in the previous section, the stories of both vessels are intricately intertwined, not only in their collaborative loss, but in the several searches that have been made for the wrecks.

The key to finding the *U-550* was the *Pan-Pennsylvania.* The discovery of the tanker in 1994 provided a starting point for anyone who intended to search for the U-boat. Yet the direction in which to go from that starting point was unknown.

For the 1994 search for the *U-550* and *Pan-Pennsylvania*, we checked the hang numbers with a depth recorder. Joe opted to search for the U-boat by means of side-scan sonar. The difference between these electronic detection devices is enormous.

The depth recorder shoots a cone-shaped signal straight down to the seabed. The deeper the water, the larger the area of the cone that reaches the bottom. Picture the cone as an upside-down ice cream cone. If the cone encounters an object – reef, rock, or shipwreck – the target shows on the screen as a spike. The downside of a depth recorder is that the boat must pass almost directly over the target in order for it to register.

The side-scan sonar fish operates differently. Its sensors scan sideways from both sides of the towfish, hence the name. The sonar array is towed behind the boat on a cable that is long enough to enable the fish to "fly" slightly above the seabed. Depending on the sensitivity of the sonar array, it can scan as far as a quarter mile to either side.

A depth recorder may be all that is needed for a known wreck site

Clockwise from upper left: underwater and upside down; after acid bath; on deck; after final polish.

or a cluster of hang numbers. But a side-scan sonar unit is necessary to search a broad swath of ocean. Furthermore, whereas a depth recorder can be purchased for a few hundred dollars, a side-scan sonar unit costs tens of thousands of dollars. Not only that, but whereas any good skipper can learn to read a depth recorder screen, a skilled sonar operated is needed to operate the fish (and keep it from crashing into the seabed) and interpret the images that mark the screen or print-out.

So Mazraani and his cohorts hired Garry Kozak and rented his side-scan sonar unit. When it came to searching for shipwrecks, Garry was one of the two most highly skilled sonar operators in the United States (the other being Vince Capone). The gang went to sea with high hopes. But after two days of towing the fish back and forth across pre-laid grid lines, they found nothing.

The next step was a visit to the National Archives in College Park, Maryland. Joe, Steve Gatto, and Brad Sheard delved into the official records from World War Two. Archival research can be the most boring occupation that you can possibly imagine. You can spend hours – even days – in going through reams of documents that may be hand written and difficult to read, or poorly inked carbon copies whose typewritten text is faint and faded, or thousands of pages of records that have nothing to do with the object of your search except that they are kept in the same box with records that you *are* searching for. Research is usually hit or miss, with misses outstripping the hits.

But it takes only one "Eureka!" to make every hour of boredom worthwhile. In this case, the eureka was the deck log of the *SC-1338*: a sub chaser that was dispatched to the *Pan-Pennsylvania* because the inverted and the largely submerged hull was drifting with the current with its bow still afloat. This meant that the wreck site that we dived in 1994 was not located at the original action site, but was miles away when the hull finally lost enough of its buoyancy to sink.

The *SC-1338* stayed with the drifting wreck until it finally gave up the ghost. A buoy was deployed over the wreck site in order to mark it as a hazard to navigation. To locate the action site, where the U-boat sank, Joe, Steve, and Brad had to backtrack the course of the sub chaser in the opposite direction of the tanker's drift. This system would not pinpoint the site of the U-boat, but it would provide a general idea of where it sank.

After creating a new grid pattern for the most likely area of the U-boat's location, they contacted Garry Kozak again. Garry was busy at the time with other work at the time, so there was a month's delay before he could make himself available. After another two days of towing the fish, they found two targets: the first one was too large to be a U-boat, but the second one appeared to be about the right size. The depth of the second target was 300 feet.

Steve Gatto, who contributed significantly to this chapter, told me, "It was late in the day and getting dark, with no time to do a dive; plus bad weather was coming in so we needed to leave. We decided to put my drop camera in the water and after several passes of just missing the target we started seeing cod and pollack, then steel structure and we all shouted at the same time when we saw a hatch. We weren't sure if it was the forward or aft hatch but more important it was a confirmed submarine. Approximately a week later we returned and Joe, Tom, myself, and Brad" made a dive to check it out – and landed on the conning tower of the long lost U-boat.

In addition to Joe Mazraani, onboard on the discovery trip were Steve Gatto, Tom Packer, Brad Sheard, Eric Takakjian, and Anthony Tedeschi.

But there's more! As noted above, by reaching out through the Internet, they made contact with a number of associated individuals: three survivors of the *U-550*; one son each of two survivors of the *U-550*; the grandson of another *U-550* survivor; the granddaughter of a sailor of the *Joyce*, who said that her grandfather was still alive at the age of 92; a sailor of the *Gandy*; a survivor of the *Pan-Pennsylvania*; and through these people there came information about others. The list goes on.

Surviving *U-550* member Robert Ziemer recalled that every sailor had exited from the sinking U-boat. Hugo Renzmann agreed, saying that he checked to make sure that everyone escaped from inside the pressure hull. They all wore life vests and escape lungs. They stood either on the conning tower or on the forward deck as the U-boat settled beneath the waves. One by one, they slipped into the water and swam toward the nearest destroyer escort. But the destroyer escort got underway and left most of the German sailors in the water. The *Joyce* rescued thirteen men, one of whom later died of his injuries. The rest of the German sailors were left to their fate. Their fate was death: a lingering demise that was long in coming as they floated on the sea while waiting to be rescued by their enemy sailors.

This dramatic and horrible eventuality contradicted the one that the Allies had suggested when they recovered drifting bodies several weeks after the *U-550* sank. Those dead Germans plus others who were never found had not escaped from the sunken U-boat as it rested on the bottom, but had floated in the hot sun until their strength gave out. Thus they suffered the same fate to which the Nazi U-boat arm accorded to thousands of Allied merchant mariners whose ships were torpedoed and whose survivors were left to die at the caprices of the wide, wide sea.

On a subsequent trip, Joe and his team returned to the area and dived on the first target: the one that was too big to be a U-boat. It turned out to be the stern section of the *Pan-Pennsylvania* – twenty miles from the forward section that was discovered in 1994. I suppose that this qualifies as a twofer.

Down Deep

Bob Meimbreese is the owner and skipper of the *Down Deep*. Strictly speaking, his boat does not qualify as a privately-owned non-charter boat, as he habitually charters the boat for both fishing and diving trips. But Bob is also willing to take a chance on finding undeclared shipwrecks whenever the opportunity presents itself. By doing so he wiggled sideways into the category. I for one am grateful for his open-mindedness in this regard

The beginning of this story goes back a long way: to 1986. The ending did not come about until 2007: twenty-one years of searching, diving, and identifying. As the saying goes, Rome wasn't built in a day. Sometimes the span between a shipwreck's discovery and its identification is a long one. Here is a case in point.

To understand the generation of this story, we need to go to 1986. That was when Homer Pratt, skipper of the *Ursula*, along with his son Johnny, accidentally ran over a previously unknown wreck site southeast of Cape May, New Jersey, while returning from a fishing trip to the Baltimore Canyon. Pratt noted the loran coordinates for future reference.

That autumn, on October 20, when a group of divers chartered the *Ursula* to dive on the recently discovered Offshore Paddle Wheeler (since identified as the *Admiral Dupont*, but that's another story), he suggested investigating the new site instead. Most "first" dives turn out to be unidentifiable snags or the splayed out remains of wooden barges, which are boring to dedicated wreck-divers except for the unharvested lobster population. The group demurred for a while, then finally yielded to persuasion.

Roger Fehrle provided me with the names (and the spellings) of those who made this historic first dive: Dave Andrews, Ward Bubeck, Joe Dobarro, Warren Dagrosa, Mike Edge, Pat Farrel, Roger Fehrle, Bobbin Ferrin, Caitland Freels, George Gillispie, Bill Kuppel, Bill Sykes, and Ken Williams.

Upon descending to a depth of 160 feet, the divers were delighted to find the remains of an ancient screw steamer that was laid out perfectly on the bottom. The hull was largely broken down, but it was contiguous from bow to stern. Each end was recognizable. An iron propeller graced the tall standing stern, the engine and boilers protruded high above the surrounding wreckage, and the bow was flattened but clearly distinguishable. The propeller shaft was exposed from the rear of the engine to the front of the poop deck because the decks had collapsed around it. Portholes and other brass artifacts abounded.

Because of the trove of relics that were recovered on the discovery dive, and the skipper who had convinced the divers to check out the site, the wreck was dubbed "Homer's Hot Spot."

Despite subsequent sporadic trips to the wreck, Homer's Hot Spot remained unidentified for the next six years. Then, on July 26, 1992,

Mike Edge recovered the builder's plaque on which the names of the vessel and her builder were stamped: *Charles Morand*. The *Charles Morand* sank after colliding with the schooner *Zacheus Sherman*. Ironically, Mike recovered the identifying relic exactly one hundred and two years to the day after the *Charles Morand* was lost.

Let us go back a century, to July 26, 1890. Headed south was the steamer *Charles Morand*, bound from New York City to Newport News, Virginia, thence to Vera Cruz, Mexico. Her cargo consisted of case oil. Proceeding north was the *Zacheus Sherman*, a schooner en route from Baltimore, Maryland to Salem, Massachusetts. Her holds were filled with coal.

A converging course brought both vessels together in a fog. One source gave the location of the collision site as "fifty miles northeast of the *Delaware* Lightship." Another source stated that the collision occurred "off the Capes of Delaware during a heavy gale." Yet another source claimed that the two vessels collided off Fenwick Island, Delaware. Obviously, neither of the participants knew for certain where they were located at the time of the encounter.

The bow of the schooner drove into the side of the steamship with devastating force. The schooner's cutwater was carried away, her port bow plates were stove in, and she commenced to leak prodigiously, requiring her pumps to operate at "about 100 strokes per hour."

The two vessels drifted apart in the fog and lost sight of each other. Neither master knew the name of the vessel with which he had collided.

The *Charles Morand* fared worse than the schooner. She was abandoned five minutes after the collision. "The captain, his wife and daughter and all the crew were picked up in two boats [on the] 26th, 11 AM, off *Five Fathom Bank* Lightship and landed at Boston [Massachusetts] on the 27th by steamer *D L Miller*. Captain Marshall is slightly injured."

The badly damaged schooner was later picked up by the tug *Battler*, and towed to Jersey City, New Jersey for temporary repairs. They arrived on the 28th. Captain Babb, master of the *Zacheus Sherman*, reported no deaths or injuries.

Although Captain Marshall reported that the *Charles Morand* had sunk shortly after the collision, at the time this did not appear to have been the case. On July 30, it was reported in New York City that "Capt. Winnett of the ocean tug *Talisman*, which arrived here [New York City] from Charleston [South Carolina] with two scows in tow, reports that July 28, when thirteen miles northeast of Absecom Lighthouse, he passed a partially-submerged wreck, which appeared to be either a steamer or a barge with pole masts. The wreck seemed to be a very dangerous one, as it was lying directly in the path of coastwise vessels. It was probably the steamer *Charles Morand*."

Now that the location of the *Charles Morand* is precisely known, we know that the derelict that was spotted by Captain Winnett must have been a different wreck.

As chance would have it, Gene Peterson had a charter scheduled on the *Down Deep* three days after Homer's Hot Spot was identified. I was signed up for the charter. When we arrived at the Cape May dock on the morning of July 29, we had no intention of going to the *Charles Morand*, because the location had not yet been disseminated. However, Bob Meimbreese informed us that he had obtained some wreck numbers from Jim Bowen, skipper of the lobster boat *Wayward*, and that the *Charles Morand* was among them. He asked us if we wanted to go there instead of to our intended destination.

It took only the blink of an eye for us to change our plans. Once on site, Gene and I went down first to set the hook. We then circumnavigated the wreck. Visibility was about thirty feet ambient, so we had a good look at the site. We exchanged shrugs when we returned to the anchor line. Although the depth was right, the wreck did not fit the description of the *Charles Morand* that we had been given. It was obvious to both of us that this wreck belonged to a much later era: no earlier than World War One, and possibly as late as World War Two.

We had discovered a previously undived shipwreck!

Because we found no significant artifacts, I christened the site Bob's Cold Spot. As other divers started to visit the wreck, it collected a host of aliases: the Unknown Freighter, Dudley's Freighter, and the Ice Cream Cone.

Artifacts were recovered on subsequent trips, but none that helped to identify the wreck. And there matters remained for the next two years.

On July 4, 1994, I was diving with Tom Packer on Bob's Cold Spot when I spotted a dark shape some fifty feet off the port side of the wreck. I swam across the white sandy bottom to investigate. What I found was a disarticulated chunk of wreckage that was shrouded in fishing nets. Under the netting I saw several portholes and, after close examination, the helm's brass stand. I had discovered the wheelhouse wreckage!

I signaled frantically with my light. Tom saw the wagging beam and raced across the open sand to my side. I showed him the helm stand and portholes. He was ecstatic. It was too late in the dive to fill liftbags, so we sadly returned to the anchor line empty-handed.

Because the wreck was so far offshore, we had planned to make only one deep dive, then come inshore to dive on a shallow wreck which had been discovered several weeks before. Eight minutes into the repetitive dive, I found a brass triangle protruding from the sand next to the engine. The dimensions were barely more than an inch long on each side. I fanned sand away with one hand while I wiggled the thin brass sheet with the other. It took very little effort to free the relic. I drew it straight out until I found myself hold a sheet of brass that measured a foot in length and two and a half inches in width.

Regular shapes like letters were cut out of the sheet, in the fashion of a stencil. I held it up to the light that beamed down from the surface, and read "S. S. CLEOPATRA E. D." Positive identification!

I had written about the 1899 collision between the *Cleopatra* and the *Crystal Wave* in *Shipwrecks of Delaware and Maryland*. Neither wreck had been located at the time of publication, in 1990. I updated the relevant chapters when I revised the book in 2002. I presume that "E.D." stands for "engine department," as that was where I located the stencil.

Ever since that day, whenever I talk about shipwreck identification with my wreck-diving buddies, I say, "I always go for the stencil." The replies consist of sour faces and groans.

To return to Bob's Cold Spot, which we did the following day, I dived with John Moyer because Tom had to work. After hooking into the wreck, I led John to the wheelhouse wreckage. We did what we could to free the stand from the debris, and ran a guideline to the anchor line. Gene Peterson and Lynn DelCorio went down next, secured two 500-pound liftbags to the helm stand, and inflated them. The positive buoyancy broke the stand free from the surrounding debris, and raised it about ten feet off the bottom, but there it hung – held by the net like a bug in a spider web. The addition of another liftbag did not break the stand free. They tied a sisal line to the stand, and reeled the line to the boat's anchor line. After decompressing, they brought the line to the boat so there was a direct route to the stand.

John and I had not planned to make a repetitive deep dive. But we certainly were not about to leave the stand where it was hanging. We followed the new guideline to the helm stand. I took photographs while John secured a safety line to the stand. John backed away. I circled the shroud of netting, cutting one strand at a time with my dive knife. When I was down to the last strand, I tucked my gauge panel and mesh bag close to my chest. I extended my arm as far as I could reach. I looked back and nodded at John, who was holding the decompression reel in both hands, and delicately sliced through the last strand that entangled the helm. In a huge cloud of sand and mud, the helm stand exploded toward the surface like a Titan missile launched from a nuclear submarine. I never even saw it go.

John and I return to the anchor line with the safety line in hand. We ascended to our decompression stops, which fortunately were not too long because our bottom time had been relatively short. We saw the helm stand drift past us to the boat, where Gene and Lynn secured a line to it.

It took all five of us (includ-ing Bob) to haul the heavy stand out of the water, up the ladder, over the transom, and onto the deck.

Gene expressed an interest in displaying the helm in his dive shop, Atlantic Divers. In fact, as if in prescience, he had mentioned that to me on the evening after the trip on which I found the stand, when I slept at his house. I thought his shop was a prime location for public display. So he took the helm home, cleaned it, and stood it prominently in the shop for all his customers to see.

I entertained the hope that the cover of the stand had writing that would lead to the identification of the wreck, the way the helm stand that I recovered in 1973 from the *Ioannis P. Goulandris* had identified the wreck. When Gene cleaned the stand, he did find lettering stamped on the cover: "John Hastie Co. Ltd, Patented Greenock," and a serial number: "2705".

Unfortunately, the stamping referred to no ships that were known to have been lost in the area. And that is where matters stood . . . for thirteen years.

In 2007, Gene decided to use the Internet to conduct research about the manufacturer of the helm stand. He quickly ascertained that the John Hastie Company was located in Scotland. From the Glasgow University Archives, he learned that the company furnished steering gear to local shipbuilders. As steering gear technology evolved, the company used the same serial number three times: once for screw gear, once for steam gear, and once for hydraulic gear.

The dates for the screw steering gear were too early for the wreck, while the dates for the hydraulic steering gear were too late. That left the steam steering gear, the item in question having been shipped to Swan Hunter & Wigham in 1920, where two sister ships were then under construction: the *St. Mary* and the *Miraflores*.

The *St. Mary* burned and sank in the Mississippi River in the 1950's, and was subsequently scrapped. The *Miraflores* disappeared without a trace after departing from Haiti on February 14, 1942. She never reached her destination, which was New York City. The fate of her thirty-four hands was unknown; they were reported missing and presumed dead.

Gene learned that secondary German sources credited *U-432*, Kapitanleutnant Heinz-Otto Schultze, with sinking the *Miraflores* on February 19, 1942, in a grid square that approximated the location of Bob's Cold Spot.

Hats off to Gene for a fine piece of research!

The U.S. Navy kept records of all vessels that were lost or attacked in what was known during the war as the Eastern Sea Frontier, an operational area that extended from Maine to northern Florida, and to a distance of one hundred miles from shore. The *Miraflores* did not appear in the war diary of the ESF. This accounts for how I missed the *Miraflores* when I wrote *Track of the Gray Wolf*. The ESF war diary was my primary source of information relating to vessels that were lost in the area.

After the war, the Allies established an Assessment Committee to comb German records for the purpose of establishing which U-boat sank which Allied vessel, and which Allied warships and aircraft should receive credit for sinking which U-boat. Again, there was no mention of the *Miraflores* in American records.

This gave me pause to wonder what latter-day German researchers thought they knew that the Assessment Committee had missed. Since the National Archives has microfilms of U-boat deck logs, I decided to look at the log of the *U-432* for the period in question. What I found added ambiguity to an already puzzling story.

According to the records, Schultze sank the *Olinda* off the Virginia Capes on the night of February 18, 1942. The name is actually typed in the deck log. Schultze knew for certain the name of the vessel because the skipper was taken aboard the U-boat for interrogation. Captain Benemond was then released. The USS *Dallas* rescued the entire crew after they spent an uncertain night at sea. The wreck of the *Olinda* has not been found.

Eight hours later, Schultze noted in his log an attack on a 4,000-ton merchant vessel. No name was given. It is this entry on which the credit for sinking the *Miraflores* was based. Yet somehow the Allied Assessors overlooked this entry. On the other hand, the Assessors credited Schultze with sinking the *Norlavore* six days later, when there is no log entry to corroborate it, simply because he was in the area in which the Assessors believed the *Norlavore* sank with all hands.

The speculation that is currently in vogue adds the *Miraflores* tonnage to Schultze's credit, but subtracts the *Norlavore* tonnage: 2,158 tons instead of 2,677 tons.

So who was right – the contemporary Assessors or recent German researchers? I dislike taking sides in a debate that is shrouded by so much opacity. But if I had to render an expert opinion, I would give Schultze credit for sinking the *Miraflores*, and take away credit for sinking the *Norlavore*.

No matter who is right or who is wrong, I don't think it mattered to the thirty-four men who lost their lives in the sinking of the *Miraflores*, or to the twenty-eight men who died in the sinking of the *Norlavore*. When all is said and done, human lives are more important than tonnage statistics. That is a cross that the Nazis refused to bear in their bid for world domination.

On a personal level, I wish that Gene had found this information a year earlier, before I published *The Fuhrer's U-boats in American Waters*. Then I could have incorporated this previously unknown story in the text and appendices.

It only goes to show that shipwreck research is never-ending.

Never-ending is right. Gene continued his research on the *Miraflores*, and uncovered some interesting facts. The *Miraflores* measured 270 feet in length. She was owned by the Standard Fruit Company. Her cargo usually consisted of tropical fruits such as bananas, coconuts, and cashews, which she transported from Central American ports to New Orleans, Louisiana. After the U.S. entry into World War Two, Captain Charles Thompson, master, was ordered to proceed to Haiti for additional cargo, thence to New York City. This change in orders unwittingly placed the *Miraflores* on a converging course with a German torpedo.

According to Gene, "at 3:18 a.m. Schultze positioned his submarine perpendicular to the little fruit ship steaming north and fired two torpedoes. Both struck the freighter with a united explosive power. The first torpedo struck forward of the wheelhouse cutting the ship in two which left the bow intact. The second followed striking amidship obliterating the stern forward of the aft deck house. It is probable that this enormous explosion caused the S.S. *Miraflores* to sink within a few minutes. The possibility of the crew escaping the doomed sinking ship was nil. Had anyone survived the tremendous blast, the icy cold water and confusion in darkness diminished all hopes of escape to less than a few minutes. Hypothermia would spare no one in such an inhospitable frigid sea so far from land. No distress call could be made due to the direct and devastating blast near the bridge that probably stunned or killed all officers and crew in that proximity instantly."

The *U-432* suffered a similar fate a year later. "After sinking the *Miraflores*, Schultze and the *U-432* continued to plunder the American shipping route. The U-boat torpedoed the *Azalea City* farther off the New Jersey coast on February 21 and then the *Marore* off North Carolina before crossing the Atlantic to La Pallice, France to resupply. Three more successful patrols under Schultze were made by the *U-432* on convoys in the north Atlantic.

"On March 11, 1943, the *U-432* was detected by ASDIC of the Free French corvette *Aconit*. The *U-432's* success was soon to end. The crew under the new command of Hermann Eckhardt was celebrating the sinking of HMS *Harvester* of convoy HX-228. Failing to observe the corvette, the *U-432* was taken off guard and machine gunned killing several crew including Eckhardt. *U-432* was then accidentally rammed during a boarding attempt and sank. Twenty-six crewmembers were lost and 20 were captured, interrogated and then spent the remainder of the war as POWs."

After commanding the *U-432*, Schultze took command of the *U-849*. On November 25, 1943, the *U-849* sank with all hands in the South Atlantic, by depth charges that were dropped from an American B-24 Liberator.

Gene related other parts of the story via his online dive shop newsletter:

"The wreck is 53 miles southeast of Cape May in 165 feet of water. In 1992 Bill Dumeze the captain of the red hulled clammer *Arlene Snow* ran over a snag while fishing. He contacted Jim Bowen an avid wreck fisher and the two left Cape May inlet following only a compass bearing to the wreck site. Jim believed this was going to be some wild goose chase because Bill had recorded no loran numbers. After four long hours steaming at 12 knots to the middle of nowhere Captain Bill told Jim to slow the boat down and follow his bearings as he scanned the bottom finder. After what seemed to be a convoluted course of bearing changes over a period of a half hour, Bill shouted to drop a buoy. Jim Bowen looked over Bill's shoulders as a large spike appeared on the screen that looked like an ice cream cone with a sprinkle of jimmies. These were in fact fish hovering over the virgin wreck. Jim was amazed that any one could find a wreck scanning a depth recorder with no land bearings. Bill explained that clammers and scallopers know the bottom of the ocean well spending 99% of their time looking at the depth recorder searching for their harvest. Jim gave the wreck its first nick name the Ice Cream Cone."

Gene advertised the identification on several war memorial sites. He professed his interest in contacting surviving family members. Eventually he made contact with one former crewmember, with a grandson of the vessel's carpenter, and with a great-granddaughter of another crewmember.

The former crewmember was Walter Autry. He joined the merchant marine service at the age of 17. He served aboard the *Miraflores* for a year in the capacity of a fireman. He left the *Miraflores* in 1940 in order to join the U.S. Navy. He attended diesel school in 1941, then spent the war aboard naval vessels that operated in the Pacific Theater.

Gene sent Autry a piece of wood that he recovered from the wreck. This piece of wood became Autry's most cherished possession.

David Shields, grandson of the vessel's carpenter, called Gene on the phone and chatted about the grandfather he never knew. Gene sent him a piece of wood, too.

Karen Magill's great-grandfather was John Jule Brockerville. Gene struck up a correspondence with her, and sent her a packet that contained an account of the wreck's discovery and subsequent identification.

Karen wrote to Gene, "I am overwhelmed and in tears looking at the photographs and reading the stories within the links you have so graciously provided to me. I cannot express how happy my family will be to see these!

"My great-grandfather, John Jule Brockerville, was born on October 24, 1889 on an island called St. Pierre (a small island owned by France, just off the coast of Newfoundland). He was named after his father, Jean Gilles Broqueville, who was born in Cancale, France on October 20, 1863 and was lost at sea 19th of December 1892. Shortly afterward, his mother moved from the island over to Newfoundland, to a small fishing village called Roundabout, where my grandfather Gregory Joseph Brockerville was born (August 20, 1912). The family eventually re-settled in Lawn, Newfoundland, my family's hometown. Lawn is located on the very southern tip of Newfoundland, on the Burin Peninsula, in Placentia Bay. My grandfather also was a sailor in WWII, but for the Canadian Navy.

"During World War I, Newfoundland was still under British rule and was not yet part of Canada. My great-grandfather enlisted with the Royal Navy and served on various ships throughout the war. I have attached his naval records, which I obtained from over in the U.K. His enlistment papers show his place of birth as Marystown, which is a town near our village in Newfoundland. I can only assume it was easier to enlist and get payment if you stated your birthplace as British (Newfoundland) and not French (the island St. Pierre). He survived the Great War and returned home to Newfoundland.

"When World War II broke out, he was too old to serve, so enlisted in the Merchant Marines instead. . . . I can't begin to express to you how much all of your information and photographs are going to mean to my family. My second cousin, Earl Brockerville, in particular, has been trying for years to obtain information on his grandfather and, quite frankly, this information is going to make him a very happy man. Both Earl and myself are very avid history and genealogy buffs and, boy oh boy, I feel like I just hit the jackpot! Again, I can't thank you enough."

As Gene wrote so prophetically, "The human story of shipwrecks often exceeds our expectations. The misery that was suffered in order to maintain our freedom should never be forgotten."

Every year, Gene organizes a memorial dive to the *Miraflores*. After a moment of silence, he places flowers over the wreck site in honor of the missing crew who sacrificed their lives in the cause of freedom.

Amen.

The overall irony is that now, with the discovery of the *Octavian*, there are two previously unknown World War Two wrecks lying within a few miles of each other. Neither one made it into the history books about vessels that were torpedoed by German U-boats, including my own two books on the subject: *Track of the Gray Wolf* (1989) and *The Fuhrer's U-boats in American Waters* (2006). The present book about the *Octavian* must count as an addendum.

These two discoveries make me wonder how many other mysteries that wreck-divers will encounter and solve in the deep waters off the American eastern seaboard.

Big Mac

Harold Moyers had the *Big Mac* custom built in Maine. Under his direction, she was specifically outfitted for offshore overnight dive trips, complete with an onboard compressor under the deck. The first wreck that he discovered happened like this.

When I revised *Shipwrecks of Delaware and Maryland* in 2002, I expanded the text and added wrecks that were not included in the original book. I couldn't include every wreck that lay off Delmar – that would require a multi-volume encyclopedia. So I chose the ones that were the best-known sites, and added some that had not yet been discovered. The book exceeded my space allocation, forcing me to delete two pages of photos. One wreck that I researched but ultimately left out due to space constraints turned out to be an unfortunate omission.

In 2005, I received a phone call from Harold Moyers. He had just dived on a very old and unidentified shipwreck off the coast of Delaware, in 205 feet of water. He described the condition and lay-out of the site, and gave me the approximate location. Five minutes into the conversation, I said, "That sounds like the *Lucy Neff*. Let me check my files."

I pulled out my *Lucy Neff* folder. Everything that Harold told me matched perfectly with the *Lucy Neff*. As I am wont to say (and write), most shipwrecks are identified not by the recovery of an artifact with the name stamped on it, but by a preponderance of evidence. I was convinced that Harold had found the *Lucy Neff*, as it was the only large steamer that was known to have been lost in that area.

Photo by Steve Gatto

The next trip to the *Lucy Neff* was aboard the *Explorer*. Captains Rusty Cassway and Brian Sullivan. Brian was not aboard when Steve Gatto recovered the builder's plaque. The information that was stamped in bronze confirmed my conviction. Positive ID.

Photo by Steve Gatto

The *Lucy Neff* was a wooden-hulled steamship that was built in 1893 by James Davidson in West Bay City, Michigan. She possessed the profile of a typical Great Lakes steamer, with the machinery aft and the wheelhouse above the forecastle. Her triple expansion reciprocating steam engine could generate 92 nominal horsepower. She measured 225 feet in length, 37 feet abeam, and 13.5 feet in depth of hold. Her tonnage was registered at 946 gross tons, 759 net tons. Her two masts were schooner rigged. Her original name was *W. P. Ketcham*, at which time she was owned and operated by the Ketcham Steam Ship Company. Her home port was Chicago, Illinois.

So much for construction statistics. The *W. P. Ketcham* started her career as an inland freighter. She plied the freshwater waves of the Great Lakes for nine years without recorded incidents. During this time her primary cargoes were coal, lumber and pulpwood.

The *W. P. Ketcham* changed hands in 1902, when she was sold to Sidney Neff & Son. In honor of the new company's ownership, she was duly renamed *Lucy Neff*, likely after a family member: a common practice both then and now. She continued serving on the Inland Lakes trade until 1907. At that time she was sold again. Her new owner was the C. L. Dimon-Coast Transit Company, which conducted business in the oceanic transport trade. They retained the *Lucy Neff*'s name. Her first foray as a "salty" found her San Francisco bound – and bound for trouble.

A series of newspaper accounts best described the *Lucy Neff*'s travails:

March 14, 1907, "Capt. Hardig [sic] and J. M. McDonald, of the Miami Lumber Co., of San Francisco, are looking after the rebuilding of the steamers *Lucy Neff* and *Minnie E. Kelton*, which have been purchased for use on the Pacific coast."

August 29, 1907: "The steamer *Lucy Neff*, from the Great Lakes, which put into Bath, Me. [Maine], several weeks ago, leaking, will discharge her cargo of 1,100 tons of Pittsburg coal. This coal has been purchased by the Sagadahoc Light and Power Co. The *Neff* was on her way from Detroit, Mich., to San Francisco, and while coming up from Sidney, Cape Breton, commenced leaking."

February 8, 1908: "The big lake freighter *Lucy Neff*, Captain Harding, which was obliged to put into this port last July while on a trip from Detroit, Mich., to San Francisco, bade good bye to the Shipping City yesterday when she steamed down the river, the salutes of the numerous Industries bidding her a bon voyage as she started on the remainder of her long voyage.

"Owing to the amount of ice which surrounded the craft at her dock, considerable difficulty was encountered in steering her as she

Photo by
Steve Gatto

swang [sic] out into the river and the tide and mass of ice commenced to set over towards the rocks on the Woolwich shore. Capt. Harding immediately whistled for assistance and Cap. Coss of the ferryboat *Hockomock* went to her assistance and pulled her away from her perilous position until she was able to get steerage-way and no further trouble was encountered.

"The first stopping place of the *Neff* will be New York where she will take on a cargo of carbide and then she will proceed by way of the Straits of Magellan, the route recently taken by Read Admiral Evans' battleship squadron, and it is expected that in 73 days from the date of leaving New York she will reach San Francisco on her journey of 15,000 miles."

The mention of the battleship squadron referred to the round-the-world cruise of America's Great White Fleet: sixteen battleships that were painted white, in President Teddy Roosevelt's show of naval strength. The expedition lasted from December 16, 1907 to February 22, 1909. The passage of the *Lucy Neff* took nearly as long.

February 19, 1908: "A dispatch from New York announces the arrival of the steamer *Lucy Neff* from Detroit, Mich., via Bath, Me. [Maine], bound for San Francisco. This contradicts the story which emanated from Cleveland [Ohio] last month that the steamer had been wrecked on an island in the south Atlantic. The unfortunate craft must have been some other steamer. The *Lucy Neff* was formerly owned by the late Capt. Sidney O. Neff of Milwaukee and is well known on Lake Superior. After she was sold to Pacific coast parties, she was given her salt water equipment at Detroit. She left there for the Atlantic some time last summer, and has been in the coast trade."

February 20, 1908: "Capt. Harding arrived here on the 11th from Bath, Maine, and was berthed at the Erie Basin [Brooklyn, New York]. The *Lucy Neff* left Detroit last spring for San Francisco and met with such a buffeting after leaving the St. Lawrence that she had to put into Bath where she spent several months undergoing repairs. She is one of the several steamers which were purchased on the Lakes for the Pacific coast trade. She is to load a cargo of carbide."

June 9, 1908: "The American steamer *Lucy Neff*, Captain Harding, out 122 days from Bath, Me., for San Francisco with 500 tons of carbide, arrived here [Oakland, California] this morning with a broken crank shaft to her propeller. Repairs will be made here."

The *Lucy Neff* eventually reached San Francisco after more than a year and three months, spent either at sea or in various ports undergoing repairs. November 25, 1909: "The steamer *Lucy Neff*, a lake-built vessel, which was brought out to the Pacific a few years ago and subsequently laid up for a long time, is again in service."

June 18, 1910 (Los Angeles): "The steamer *Lucy Neff*, Captain Klitgard, arrived today from San Diego with 450,000 feet of lumber loaded at Everett [near Seattle, Washington], for the Southern California Lumber Company."

She continued to serve in the lumber trade for the next several years. By this time the steamer had been fitted with a newfangled device called wireless.

In 1913, the *Lucy Neff* found herself working between ports in the Gulf of Mexico and the U.S. eastern seaboard. According to the *Lloyd's Register of Ships*, her new owner of record was one of her previous owners: C. L. Dimon of New York City. Oddly, her port of registry was still given as San Francisco.

To complicate ownership matters even more, a newspaper article that was published on December 6, 1915, notes not only that ownership changed hands once again, but that the *Lucy Neff* was embroiled in an international political upheaval. "Great Britain's latest interference with American trade and manufactures is an embargo on logwood from Jamaica. This not only affects the dyestuffs industry but seriously interferes with the manufacture of silk, cotton and woollens [sic].

"One of the firms most seriously hampered is the Oakes Manufacturing Company of Long Island City, dealers in dye materials. The embargo caught this firm's steamship the *Lucy Neff* loading 1,000 tons of wood at Jamaica. The vessel would have sailed on Monday [December 6, 1915].

"Because of the lack of German dyes [due to the onset of the Great War in 1914] there has been a great demand for the whole vegetable dyes. From logwood are obtained black, blues and browns. . . . It is thought the embargo was ordered in an attempt to force down the price for the benefit of Great Britain."

Diplomatic intervention managed to avert an international incident. The *Lucy Neff* was cleared to depart, but much to her disadvantage, for her valuable cargo never reached its destination.

December 18, 1915: "Ten minutes after Captain Langhorne and his crew of eighteen men had been taken aboard the British steamship *Chasehill* from the American vessel *Lucy Neff*, twenty miles east of Fenwick Island, off the Delaware coast, the ship they had left sank.

"The *Chasehill* had sighted the signals of distress of the *Lucy Neff* and arrived in the very nick of time.

"The *Lucy Neff* had battled for eight days against a tempest which

From the collection of Steve Gatto.

"ALL I NEED NOW IS FOR SOMEBODY TO CRITICIZE MY FIST."

The accompanying cartoon was inspired by Art Ericson (70-SSGP - W1NF) who sent one of the early distress calls using SOS, when CQD was becoming obsolete.

The badly listing lumber schooner LUCY NEFF required acrobatics on the part of this radio operator to "hang on" during this episode about 1913 off the Florida coast.

Art says he has been a ham since 1902, and now holds an Extra Class ticket. He is 86 years young.

at times blew with almost hurricane violence. The ship left Falmouth, Jamaica, December 6, laden with logwood intended for American dye-workers. From the first day she encountered boisterous weather. Last Wednesday the vessel sprank [sic] a leak. While the crew was making every effort to repair that leak another one was discovered, and it soon became apparent that the ship could not long be kept afloat.

"The nineteen men got a boat over the leeward, although they doubted that so small a craft could last very long in such a storm. Life lines were thrown out from the *Chasehill* and the shipwrecked crew were pulled aboard one after the other and made comfortable. The *Chasehill* arrived here [New York City] yesterday and anchored in the bay, off the Statue of Liberty."

It is ironic that the British first prevented the *Lucy Neff* from departing from Jamaica, then rescued her crew while their vessel was sinking.

Later, by backtracking the site's lineage, I learned more about the way in which cooperating divers passed the wreck's location from person to person. The location entered the wreck-diving realm when long-time diver Sammy Still obtained the location from commercial angler Lars Axelson, after the latter dredged up some blackened wood. Sammy owned and operated the dive boat Samar out of Wildwood, New Jersey. Sammy decided that the wreck was too deep for him to dive, so he passed along the location to Bill Tattersall.

Bill owned and operated the dive boat *Mister Ike* out of Indian River Inlet, Delaware. Although the wreck lay deeper than Bill wanted to go, he and dive buddy Mark Butler touched the wreck in 1998. Bill described the wreck as cold, dark, and deep.

After Rusty Cassway and Brian Sullivan obtained the dive boat *Explorer*, Bill gave the location to them. At that time they were not ready to dive to 200 feet, so they gave the location to Harold Moyers. And the rest, as they say, is history.

When I checked my hang log, I learned that corresponding hang numbers were on Van Strickler's list. Van was a trawler skipper who operated out of Virginia Beach, Virginia. He exchanged hang numbers with other trawler and dragger skippers all along the eastern seaboard. Van compiled a computer list which he gave to me in 1994, after I gave him all the hang numbers that I had collected from various sources throughout the years. Many hang locations on Van's list corresponded not to a single hang, but to a number of hangs from boats that hung the wreck from different directions, thus creating a cluster of numbers, one cluster of which surrounded the *Lucy Neff*. Who hung the wreck for the very first time is anyone's guess.

Another highlight of Harold Moyers and the *Big Mac* concerned the tanker *Bow Mariner*. I covered the sinking of the *Bow Mariner* in detail in *Shipwreck Sagas*. There is no need to repeat that sad story here. What is relevant in the present context is that, after the Coast Guard completed its underwater survey of the tanker's remains, and annotated the damage that was crucial to the findings that were printed in the investigative report, the *Big Mac* was the first boat to visit the site and put recreational divers onto the wreck. And Harold personally was the first one on the wreck because he made the tie-in dive.

Moyers told me, "The hook landed in the very top of the mast. I tied in. In the wheelhouse on my first dive I found and took the Alpha flag from its compartment on the port side. I wanted the international diver down flag."

Also on that first trip were Steve Gatto, Jon Hulburt, Bart Malone, Greg Masi, Mark Nix, and Tom Packer. The date was April 10, 2004. The main deck stood at 200 feet, and the after superstructure rose to 160 feet. On Harold's third trip to the wreck, my depth gauge registered a depth of 250 feet on the sand at the twin bulbous bows. Later, Steve Gatto recovered a compass but the liftbag broached on the surface, and sank alongside the bridge; when he went back down to re-inflate the liftbag, he landed on the seabed at a depth of 262 feet.

Discovering twin bulbous bows was fascinating, but more important than that trip was the trip that took place ten days later. Harold organized a group recovery operation whose purpose was for everyone to work together toward photographing and recovering the ship's bell,

which hung from a davit on the bow. In addition to Harold were Steve Gatto, Jon Hulburt, Bart Malone, Tom Packer, Joe Zeisweiss, and this author. All goals were achieved. For a short time the bell hung high and dry in Harold's house, until he, as spokesperson for the group project, donated the bell to Deb Whitcraft's New Jersey Maritime Museum, in Beach Haven, New Jersey. The bell is now on display for all to see.

Perhaps of greater significance to the world in general was an incident that occurred barely two months later – on July 3, 2004 – when the *Big Mac* was instrumental in saving the lives of five anglers whose boat caught fire.

On board the *Big Mac* that day were Harold, Steve Gatto, Jon Hulburt, Bart Malone, Tom Packer, Brad Sheard, and Joe Zeisweiss. Harold was checking hang numbers and struck pay dirt. The wreck he found in 210 feet of water was the scallop boat *Tomahawk*.

After a successful day of diving, Tom was steering the boat back to the dock when he spotted smoke in the distance. He called Steve's attention to it. According to Steve, "It looked like more than a ship powering up and barking black smoke. I picked up the binoculars and put it on the target and saw flames. Tom altered course to the vessel in distress."

Harold called the Coast Guard on the radio, and asked if there were any reports of a boat on fire. The Coast Guard response was "Negative." Steve noted, "Harold took over the wheel since he was the best person to maneuver the *Big Mac* in close quarters."

As the *Big Mac* approached the blaze they saw that, in Harold's words, "A boat was completely engulfed in raging flame. The entire boat was just a floating blob of burning fiberglass. We had seven sharp eyes out for survivors and saw none." They learned later that the survivors had fired several flares, which no one had noticed. "It wasn't until we were very close did we spot the small orange life raft. Five men, 14 to 65 poured onto our deck like out of a clown car, the raft had seemed so small. They were very grateful, the sun was dropping and they were anticipating a long float. They didn't have time to get off a mayday and the EPIRB was incinerated by the fire. Divers having a notoriously dark sense of humor, we forever joked that the *Big Mac* is the only dive boat that brought more souls back than we left with!"

The name of the fiery boat was *Santa Clara*.

Not all shipwrecks (or boat wrecks) end so fortuitously with respect to the rescue of those onboard. Witness the dire circumstances of the scallop boat *Lady Mary*. She departed from Cape May, New Jersey and headed for the rich fishing grounds off the coast of Delaware.

In the pre-dawn hours of March 29, 2009, it was unlikely that everyone on the *Lady Mary* was sound asleep in his bunk, despite the crew's exhaustion after catching, loading, and cleaning five tons of scallops in a five-day period.

Of the seven men onboard the *Lady Mary* that night, four held United States Coast Guard certified captain licenses. They knew and enforced a strict watch protocol in which at any time only two members were allowed to sleep, for six hours. The rest of the crewmembers were either working the dredge, shucking scallops, or standing watch. At no time was there no lookout on watch.

Because the sole survivor, deck hand Jose Luis Arias, was on his off-watch below when catastrophe overtook the *Lady Mary*, his testimony was severely lacking in details that preceded the sinking of the scallop boat.

He heard a bang and was tossed out of his bunk as the boat was thrown sharply to port. He didn't know what was happening, but he quickly rushed to the open deck and struggled into a survival suit. No sooner had he pulled up the zipper than the boat rolled onto its side. He went overboard into the near freezing water. He managed to stay afloat because of the air that was trapped in the survival suit. He clung to a plank which provided additional flotation.

Other crewmembers were less fortunate. As Arias donned the survival suit, he spoke to a crewmember who was clutching an outdoor stanchion; the man was immobilized with fear and did nothing to save his life. Others inside the lurching boat were scrambling. A nearby trawler heard a short call for help on the radio; then nothing.

As the boat settled beneath the waves, the EPIRB (Emergency Position Indicating Radio Beacon) activated from immersion in the water, which it was designed to do, and automatically transmitted a continuous distress signal via satellite to listening Coast Guard stations. Monitoring EPIRB transmissions was a NOAA computer in Maryland. (NOAA is the National Oceanic and Atmospheric Administration.) Due to a typographical error on the EPIRB registration, the computer was unable to establish the identity of the vessel to which the EPIRB was registered. Had it done so, the Coast Guard could have notified the boat's owner, Royal Smith, Sr., and he could have directed them the general area in which the *Lady Mary* was working.

Worse yet, the first satellite that detected the signal was a high-altitude satellite, which gave a position in North Dakota. Not until an hour and twenty-seven minutes after the EPIRB start transmitting a distress signal, did a low-orbiting satellite intercept the continuous broadcast, and provide a solution for the actual position off the coast of New Jersey.

The boat's identity was irrelevant with regard to emergency dispatch. A Coast Guard helicopter could have responded immediately had the Coast Guard known where to direct it.

With the location confirmed, the air station in Atlantic City scrambled a crew and dispatched a helicopter to the EPIRB's position. The helicopter rescued Arias from the water, and recovered two bodies that were found floating nearby. Both bodies were wearing survival suits, but the zippers were not closed. Despite the frigid water, the first body that was retrieved appeared to have succumbed only recently. The second one exhibited vital signs but the crew was unable to revive the victim. Both these men were Royal Smith's sons.

Investigators concluded that the two men had been paralyzed by the cold water and subsequently drowned.

Four men remained missing.

Had it not been for the delay due technical flaws, it was possible that all seven crewmembers could have been saved.

A few days later, a NOAA vessel and crew were paid to locate the wreck site by means of side-scan sonar. Personnel deployed an ROV (remotely operated vehicle). The ROV's camera examined the wreck and identified its name by the lettering on the bow.

Nine days after the sinking, a group of volunteer divers departed from Cape May on the *Big Mac*, and headed for the site some sixty-six miles offshore. On board were wreck-divers Rusty Cassway, Steve Gatto, Jon Hulburt, Bart Malone, Joe Mazraani, Harold Moyers, Tom Packer, Brad Sheard, and Paul Whittaker. They took still photographs of the damage to the stern of the wreck, shot videotape, and recovered the only body that they found, inside the fish hold.

Volunteer personnel differed on subsequent dive trips. Additional wreck-divers included Andrew Don, Mark Nix, and Anthony Tedeschi.

For their heroic efforts, all participating wreck-divers on both the *Santa Clara* and the *Lady Mary* operations received Public Service Awards from the Coast Guard, not only for rescuing the survivors of the vessel in flames, but "for providing video and still photographs which were invaluable to the investigation of the casualty" of the scallop boat.

F/V Lady Mary   © 2009 Captain Steve Gatto

This latter statement provoked a bone of contention to the volunteer wreck-divers who worked so hard on the *Lady Mary*. Let me explain.

To investigate aircraft crashes and other aviation incidents, the National Transportation Safety Board utilizes a permanent staff of more than four hundred highly train investigators who represent a variety of technical and scientific disciplines. By way of comparison, the Coast Guard assigns a small boat investigation to a solitary officer who has no immediate jobs on his or her desk, and who can add another project to the ongoing workload. In some cases, such as that of the *Lady Mary*, the investigating officer has never conducted an investigation; this will be the first time.

Large vessels are required to carry a data recorder called a Vessel Management System. The VMS has several functions. One of these functions is to mark the vessel's location every thirty minutes. Another is record bridge conversations.

From its collective tracking systems, the Coast Guard learned that on the night of the loss of the *Lady Mary*, the container ship *Cap Beatrice* passed less than three-quarters of a mile from the wreck site of the scallop boat. This distance measured a straight line between the *Cap Beatrice's* putative course: that is, from one of the ship's recorded positions to another of the ship's recorded positions, thirty minutes later. If the ship made a course correction between those two positions, the VMS would not show the curve but a straight line. Thus the ship could have been closer to the *Lady Mary's* surface position than was indicated by the VMS.

Additionally, the wreck site was not necessarily the position of the *Lady Mary's* surface site. The *Lady Mary* could have drifted between the time she became *in extremis* and the time she ultimately sank.

Further Coast Guard investigation determined that the bulbous bow of the *Cap Beatrice* was painted the same shade of red that was found on the blue paint of the *Lady Mary's* rudder.

These facts posed the possibility of collision, the implication being that the container ship rammed the stern of the scallop boat. The gross tonnage of the *Cap Beatrice* was 26,833 tons, compared to 105 tons for the *Lady Mary*. The *Cap Beatrice* measured 728 feet in length, compared to 71 feet of the *Lady Mary's* length. A vessel the size of the *Cap Beatrice* could run down a small boat without being aware of it, especially when the bridge of the container ship was located at the stern of the hull, and the stacked layers of containers blocked the captain's view of the bow, and what might be in the water forward of the bow.

State Police divers examined the bulbous bow of the *Cap Beatrice*. They found no sign of damage or scratched paint. However, this examination was not conducted until two months after the incident, by which time the container ship had gone to Australia and back to Philadelphia, Pennsylvania. The bulbous bow could have been repaired and repainted in the meantime, or washed clean of extra paint by the sea.

The Coast Guard also had U.S. Navy divers retrieve the rudder for a closer look at the different colors of layers of paint.

The Coast Guard examined the still photos and watched the video footage that the wreck-divers took. Close observation showed that the lazarette hatch was open, and that the stern of the boat was crumpled.

The Coast Guard questioned the sole survivor. Arias had little information to offer about ongoing events because he was asleep when the boat became *in extremis*. By the time he was awakened by a loud bang and a sudden movement of the boat to port, the *Lady Mary* was already sinking.

After eight months of examination and contemplation, the Coast

Guard alleged that the *Lady Mary* sank for a combination of reasons

1 - Modifications to the boat over the years had reduced the hull's freeboard by four inches: this was due largely to pouring five tons of concrete into the water ballast tank under the fish hold, as a way to increase the stability of the hull.

2 - The lazarette hatch cover was left open despite 25-to-30-knot winds and 8-to-9-foot seas.

3 - No one was on watch when the boat was pooped and water filled the after hold, the weight of which pressed the stern below the water-line, leading to additional submergence of the hull.

4 - The bent and twisted condition of the rear components was due to the aft end striking the seabed. When the rudder got shoved into the propeller blades, some of the blue paint was scraped off to reveal the previous color red.

5 - The near-total loss of life was due to "a lack of training, lack of experience, language barriers, fatigue, vessel loading, drug use [mari-juana]."

Steve Gatto and his fellow wreck-divers reached different conclu-sions that were based on information that the Coast Guard dis-regarded:

1 - The lazarette's open hatch cover was irrelevant because the laz-arette compartment was extremely small; it was only large enough to accommodate the steering gear for emergency access; the lazarette could not hold enough water to destabilize the boat. It was only an as-sumption that the hatch cover was open before the boat was *in ex-tremis*. It might have been opened afterward in an effort to pump out the water.

2 - The bilges of the *Lady Mary* were outfitted with automatic pumps that switched on and pumped water overboard whenever the appropriate limit switch detected a high level of water.

3 - The three separate holds were outfitted with klaxons that screeched a blaring alarm whenever water reached a slightly higher level of water than that at which the bilge pumps were set to discharge water automatically. These alarms were loud enough to waken sleeping crewmembers, yet Arias made no mention of hearing them.

4 – The concrete that was poured into the *Lady Mary's* hold was compensation for the removal of heavy equipment when the boat was converted to a scallop boat. After Royal Smith, Sr., explained to a panel of Coast Guard investigators precisely how he modified the boat, some of them concurred with his assessment that its stability had been im-proved, not impaired.

5 - The stern ramp, skeg, and propeller were bent *down*, as if they had been pressed from above. Had these components been twisted out

of position when the stern of the boat struck the bottom, the skeg would have been found at the point of contact, and the propeller would have been bent *up*. Likewise, the stern ramp would have been bent *up*. Also, the rudder had broken free of the pintle and was found ten feet away from the rudderpost, attached by means of its safety chains the way trailers are secured to the hitch of a truck should the socket break free of the ball. Furthermore, three of the four propeller blades exhibited scrape marks in the same place where the propeller was jammed into the keel, demonstrating that the boat was underway and on the surface when these factors occurred, thus nullifying the Coast Guard's bottom contact scenario.

6 - The voice recorder on the bridge of the *Cap Beatrice* recorded sudden chatter among the sailors on watch during the container ship's near passing of the *Lady Mary*.

7 – The bulbous bow of the *Cap Beatrice* must have been responsible for the loud bang and sudden movement of the *Lady Mary* to port, to which Arias testified.

Despite these obvious objections, the Coast Guard investigator's version of events was the one that was accepted by the review board.

Also left out of the Coast Guard's equation was the human factor. Consider the six men who lost their lives in the catastrophe: both Royal Smith, Jr. and Timothy Smith were sons of Royal Smith, Sr.; Tarzon Smith was a cousin; and Frank Credle, Jorge Ramos, and Frank Reyes were friends.

Royal Smith, Sr. not only lost an uninsured vessel, but many of his close family members and fellow scallopers. He was left in remorse, as were the wives, children, and friends of the deceased.

Two months after the sinking, a trawler dredged up a body near the wreck site of the *Lady Mary*: presumably one of the scallop boat's crewmembers, although advanced decomposition prevented firm identification. DNA analysis confirmed that the body was that of one of the deckhands.

The bodies of the remaining deckhands were never found.

After years of use, and due to growing family matters, Harold sold the boat to his friend Sean Manni. Sean renamed her *Jersey Dragon*.

Interlude

Before I move on to the *Jersey Dragon*, I want to expound upon the help that wreck-divers have given throughout the years to Coast Guard investigators and insurance companies by diving on recently sunken vessels in order to recover bodies, photograph the wreck, examine the hull and interior, take notes of their findings, and file reports to appropriate investigative bodies. Sometimes they are paid, but most of the time they volunteer their services without any prospect of remuneration.

Wreck-divers have been especially useful for inspecting the conditions of wrecks that lie deeper than governmental divers are qualified to dive. Not only that, but wreck-divers are especially trained to dive on and survey wrecks of all kinds. Hence the appellation "wreck-diver."

The majority of wrecks that wreck-divers are called upon to scrutinize are fishing vessels. That is because of the proliferation of such vessels in near-shore waters. Coastal fishing is a huge commercial enterprise. Thus there are numerous fishing vessels at sea all the time, often overnight. The sheer quantity of fishing vessels that ply the wide, wide sea account for the high number of casualties.

The first such vessel that comes to my mind is one in which I was intimately involved: the *Muff Diver*. Captain Joe Riley ran daily fishing charters on this boat. His son Shane crewed for him. The summer day in question was a superb time to be out on the ocean: the air was clear with ten to fifteen knot winds out of the northwest, the temperature was 85° under the shaded canopy. The six men watching the troll lines lounged in the cockpit as the *Muff Diver* cruised at an easy six knots. With visibility of eight miles, Riley could see two other fishing boats in the vicinity: the *Box Lunch* and the *My Desire*. These three boats often fished together. The afternoon waned quietly. The date was August 9, 1987.

Without warning the port engine strangled, ground to a halt, and shut down. Riley turned off the starboard engine. As the boat went adrift, Shane donned a mask and fins, tied a rope around his waist, and eased into the water to inspect for damage. Riley warned the other boats to stay away: he wanted no blood in the water while his son worked under the hull.

The problem was immediately obvious: a two-and-a-half-inch hawser rope had entangled the port propeller shaft right up to the point at which it entered the hull. The hawser had been floating submerged when the *Muff Diver* ran over it. The rope had wrapped itself as tight as the stripes on a barber pole. Loose tentacles of rope dangled down.

Riley jumped into the water to further assess the damage. The propeller was undamaged, the struts unbroken; the shaft had not been pulled out of the stuffing box. But there was no way the combination manila and polypropylene hawser could be unwrapped because it was wound so tight. Taking deep breaths, Riley and Shane took turns ducking under the boat with a hacksaw in order to cut away the rope strand by strand.

They performed this grueling task for half an hour, and had nearly sliced through the last strand, when one of the passengers announced that the boat seemed to be down by the stern. Riley, still in the water, was clinging to the transom to catch his breath when a large wave picked him up and swept him aboard. He immediately tried to get the transom door back in place, but the stern was by that time underwater. Dunnage floated up from the after compartments, adding proof of the flooding of the bilges.

Another passenger, standing by the VHF radio on the flying bridge, shouted down that, although he could hear other people talking over the airwaves, he was unable to make contact. The radio was set on low power. Riley alerted the passengers that the boat appeared to be sinking, that he wanted them to don life vests, and that they should stand by on the bow. Then he scrambled up the ladder to the flying bridge and switched the radio to high power. He broke in on the conversation between the *Box Lunch* and the *My Desire*, issued a May Day and his position, and asked the two boats to stand by in case the *Muff Diver* went down. At the same time, he tossed down personal flotation devices and started the starboard engine.

Shane held onto the last dangling rope that still entangled the port propeller, so it would not get sucked into the starboard propeller. Riley put the engine in gear and eased on the power, hoping to get enough speed to put the boat on plane and drain the water that was now washing over the after deck. Then, by putting the transom door back in place, and using a 110-volt pump to suck out the after bilges, he could save the boat. But the weight of the water in the stern was too much for the straining single engine; the boat would not come up on plane. The automatic low-voltage pumps were overworked; water came in faster than they could eject it. Finally, the water rose high enough to drown out the starboard engine. Without power, the *Muff Diver* slowed to a stop.

At this point, five of the passengers stood on the bow while Shane helped one older gentleman along the gunwale between the outrigger and the cabin. Riley unzipped the forward canopy and climbed through the opening onto the bow deck. He tossed the life raft canister overboard. The life raft inflated automatically. With the painter, Riley pulled the raft back to the boat, and ordered the passengers to climb aboard.

Not one of them moved. They could not actually believe that the boat was sinking from under them. In order to set an example, Riley jumped into the raft, and ordered them in again. All five jumped in as one. Only Shane and the older man were left aboard the *Muff Diver*. The old man would not leave the boat. Finally, Riley shouted for Shane to climb aboard and leave the old man. Shane complied. Then the old man climbed over the railing and dropped down into the bobbing rubber raft. Riley cut the painter and let the raft drift away.

As the *Muff Diver's* stern went down, the bow rose until it pointed straight up at the sky. Air hissed out of the hawse pipe. The boat slid backward under the water and disappeared from view.

Both rescue craft closed on the raft. The *My Desire* picked up the survivors. The *Box Lunch* scooped floating debris out of the water. Everyone was safe.

In his written description of the casualty, Riley recommended, "all boats be standard equipped with a high water alarm." Although he saw no hull or structural damage when he was diving under the boat, the Coast Guard investigation concluded, "due to large rope on propeller shaft, it pulled shaft out of vessel's hull, loosening shaft packing and causing vessel to fill with water, founder and sink."

As the Coast Guard closed its casebook on the subject, the insurance company opened its own. The policy on the *Muff Diver* represented a disbursement of a quarter of a million dollars. Scams run rampant in the insurance business, so claim adjusters are frequently skeptical of large losses.

People often claim to have lost more than they did, or they inflate the value of their losses. Boat losses are particularly susceptible to fraud. It is comparatively easy for someone who wants to get rid of a worthless hull to strip it of everything of value, then sink it intentionally for the insurance money; or to alter and repaint a boat, sell it to someone far away, then make a false claim – that way he gets paid twice. There is also the possibility of subrogation – in the present case, by proving that Ocean Yacht was liable for faulty construction or poor workmanship. If an insurance company proves one fraud or subrogates one case out of a hundred claims, it more than pays for the cost of the investigations.

The insurance company hired Captain Larry Keen, owner of the *Gekos* (a 35-foot Maine Coaster), to establish that the *Muff Diver* actually sank where Riley said she had. The insurance company provided loran coordinates for the purported site. Keen in turn took on Jon Hulburt and this author to conduct the underwater survey. Our primary purpose was to photograph the wreck: in particular, the name on either the bow or stern.

It was October 10 when Jon and I slid down the *Gekos'* anchor line into the clear, warm water: visibility was better than fifty feet, and the bottom temperature was 63°. The grapnel lay just off the stern of the wreck. The *Muff Diver* sat upright with a slight list to port, at a depth of 228 feet. She ap-

The boat's name was painted proudly on the stern (as well as on both bows). The vessel was registered in Norfolk, Virginia. The black area on the left side of the photo is the opening through the transom, topped by a lift gate.

peared fresh and clean, almost as if she were sitting at her dock. The hull and superstructure were pure white against a white sandy bottom. Only the canopy knocked partly askew hinted at misadventure.

We found the transom door missing, just as Riley had said. The after-deck hatches were gone, probably blown off by air pressure as water rushed into the bilges and forced out the air. I crawled under the hull to inspect the propellers and shafts. Because of the list, the port shaft was buried. On the after deck we found signs of a hastily abandoned boat: rods and reels lay scattered about, lures hung ready for use.

Note the corrosion on the aluminum parts of the reel and on the front of the wooden rungs of the ladder. The circular light in the window above the sink (to the right of the reel) is the reflection of my strobe light in the cabin glass.

Closer inspection revealed deterioration. In only two months the exposed aluminum was already corroded. The heavy-duty reels were coated with what appeared to be hoarfrost, while stalagmites an inch long grew on the ladder rungs. Wood and fiberglass were unaffected.

All the electronics were nestled in their niches on the bridge, proof that this was no case of insurance fraud. The microphone dangled from its cord, just where Riley had dropped it after transmitting his SOS. A feeling of great sadness swept over me. The *Muff Diver* looked so serene that I could hardly believe that she lay in her final grave, that her position was untenable.

But so she was, and was forever to be. My photos proved to the insurance company that the *Muff Diver* had truly sunk, and that she had not been scuttled. The electronic equipment, expensive deep-water rods and reels, and personal belongings were worth some $75,000. The insurance company paid only for the hull.

The microphone is hanging by the coil cord, where Riley dropped it after notifying the Coast Guard preparatory to abandoning ship (or boat).

There have been so many small boat losses that their stories could fill a book. I will mention only a few: those in which wreck-divers were involved afterward.

The earliest such casualty on record was not a small boat but a tanker that measured 582 feet in length, and which grossed 12,723 tons: the Norwegian vessel *Stolt Dagali*, which was cut in two by the Israeli luxury liner *Shalom*, on November 26, 1964. The after third of the tanker sank in 130 feet of water off Manasquan, New Jersey, while the forward section remained afloat and was towed to port in New York City.

Wreck-diving was then in its infancy. Yet a few experienced divers made it a point to visit the wreck site. When Mike de Camp peered into a porthole, he saw the body of the stewardess pinned to the overhead by the buoyancy of her life vest. He reported his gruesome find to the Norwegian embassy. The Norwegians were extremely thankful for the information, so much so that they asked it if was possible to recover the body, and to look for others that might still be trapped inside. De Camp said that it was possible.

He then organized a body recovery operation. The group worked in turns with a crowbar to open the jammed door of the laundry room. They then towed the body through the passageways to a doorway that lead outside the wreck. This difficult chore took place nearly a month after the sinking, by which time the body was not a pretty sight. The feet and face were gone, and loose flesh sloughed off against the divers' wetsuits as they squeezed the body through the narrow doorway, brought it to the surface, lifted it onto the boat, and placed it in a body bag that had been provided by the Norwegian embassy. An undertaker took charge of the body at the dock. No other bodies were located.

The story of the tugboat *Thomas Hebert* is so long and complicated that Steve Gatto, the organizer (along with Tom Packer) of the involved and protracted recovery operation, is writing a book about the tragedy. Not to give the incident short shrift, I will touch upon only the highlights of the sad and sordid events.

The tug sank inexplicably by the stern in about one minute. Two men were washed out of the pilot house; they were the only survivors. The rest of the crew were trapped inside the hull, where they drowned. The date was March 7, 1993.

Five days later, the *Deep Adventures 3* (skipper John Larsen), transported Steve, Tom, Kevin Brennan, Jon Hulburt, and Gene Peterson to the wreck site. The depth was 139 feet; the temperature of the water was four degrees above freezing. Two teams made two dives each. Jon Hulburt shot videotape. The interior passages were choked with floating debris, and the doors were wedged in place by twisted jambs. Nonetheless, they found three bodies and recovered two of them.

Before the wreck-divers could return in order to recover the third body and to search the interior for the remaining two, a commercial diving outfit interceded. The Don Jon Marine Company forced the Coast Guard to ban the volunteers from the wreck, and to hire the Company to complete the job. Instead of scuba, the Don Jon Marine Company kept its divers tethered and furnished surface-supplied air for its divers to breathe. Disaster struck when one of the commercial divers became separated from his helmet. His mates recovered his body as well as the one that the wreck-divers had located. The Company then quit the job and left it for the wreck-divers to finish it.

Two more wreck-divers volunteered their services: George Powers and Lou Sarlo. Several days were required to locate and recover the final body, so that all the families of the deceased could have closure.

Another fishing vessel that has an interesting story was the *Alexander*. No lives were lost, but as Steve Gatto wrote, "Tom [Packer] and my photos and video helped to prosecute the crew and someone went to jail for intentionally sinking the vessel."

Other sunken vessels on which wreck-divers worked in various capacities were the FV *Adriatic*, FV *Beth Dee Bob*, FV *Bull Moose*, FV *Dream Catcher*, *Lady M.* (a cabin cruiser that burned to the waterline), FV *Mae Doris*, FV *Misty Blue*, and the FV *Moondancer*.

Whenever difficult and hazardous underwater jobs are required, wreck-divers are available to answer the call for help.

Jersey Dragon

In June of 2018, Sean Manni embarked on a three-day expedition off the coast of Maryland. The purpose of the trip was to dive on a number of hangs in the hope that they might prove to be shipwrecks. This kind of trip was always chancy. Instead of diving on known locations in order to be certain of exploring a shipwreck, they might dive on nothing but rock piles and junk heaps: a poor return for their time, effort, and money.

But, as I always say, "Only those who seek, will find."

And find they did. Sean was lucky – and I use the word "lucky" loosely, considering the time, effort, and money that was invested in making a discovery. Also on board on the discovery dive were Ryan Cooling, Kevin Kohling, Harold Moyers, Andy Skapik, and Evan Skapik. (Keep in mind that Harold used to own this boat.)

The first wreck they found looked like the hull of a sailing vessel or schooner barge. Harold described it as "very barren." They moved on.

On the next set of hang numbers, Sean dropped a shot line onto a large steel wreck that lay at a depth of 188 feet. Harold went down to tie in the shot. The shot weight landed off the wreck in what he described as "flat relief." What to his wondering eyes did appear (a paraphrased quote from *The Night Before Christmas*) but a field of loose brass portholes, six in all. He completed the tie-in, piled three of portholes next to the grapnel, then went exploring around the wreck on his DPV (a diver propulsion vehicle, or underwater scooter).

He found the engine, boilers, and propeller shaft. In the distance, about 90 feet away, he spotted the propeller. He scootered past it in search of more wreckage, but didn't find much that was exposed.

Meanwhile, the other divers made their descent and spent most of their bottom time filling liftbags and retrieving portholes.

Later, after his residual nitrogen time on the boat, Harold made a short repetitive dive. He repeated his perimeter search by zooming around the wreck on his scooter, looking unsuccessfully for the wreckage of the bow and stern. It seemed as if the only high relief was the propulsion machinery.

Harold explained to me what the group did next: "That night while laying on the bridle we discussed what we should do. The wreck seemed to match up well with the *New Orleans* in your [Gary Gentile's] book (12' 4 blade, 2 scotch boilers, single expansion engine, and a donkey boiler). It also had white rocks everywhere which was possibly the phosphorous the *New Orleans* was carrying (by crazy coincidence so was the *Octavian*). Most wanted to stay on the wreck and dive it again to measure the boilers and engine for ID. Two guys wanted to dive Sean's "Bone Wreck" that he had found 3 years ago (Sean works hard to find new wrecks). The group agreed to leave and come back next available weather window. We left because people said, 'It's everybody's trip, everybody has to do the dives they want.' True camaraderie among Sean's group (3 are high school buds). So we left the bird in the hand."

The shipwreck that they left behind was the *Octavian*.

The debris field adjacent to the *Octavian's* boiler. Note the spare tanks in the lower right corner; these contain nitrox for decompression.

© Rustin Cassway 2018

C3 - Shipwrecks Lost, Found, and Identified

Harold's initial explorations of the wreck led him to hope that it was the remains of the long lost *New Orleans*, a steamship that foundered in 1917, and whose iron hull had yet to be located or identified. This was not just a wild hope on Harold's part, but a considered extrapolation.

In the first edition of *Shipwrecks of Delaware and Maryland* (1990), I wrote, "If the wreckage of an old, iron-hulled steamship is ever found along the Delmarva Peninsula, tentative identification as the *New Orleans* can be made by measuring the boilers. The propeller measured thirteen and a half feet in diameter, with each of the four blades having a pitch of nineteen and a half. Since there is no record of salvage, the pale-yellow ore with its distinctive, rotten eggs odor, should be in abundance."

The newly found wreck had sulfur scattered over the bottom – thus the rationale for Harold's optimism that finally the wreck of the *New Orleans* had been discovered.

Life moves incredibly fast in today's world of modern technology. Sometimes it moves quite literally at the speed of light. As soon as Sean docked the *Jersey Dragon*, he used his smartphone to photograph the discovery team and the five recovered portholes, then immediately posted the pictures on Facebook for all his Facebook friends to see.

One person who saw and took advantage of the discovery's announcement was Rusty Cassway. He had known Sean for years. Both his boat and Sean's were docked in Cape May, New Jersey. Rusty knew the approximate area in which Sean intended to search, but not the specific location. He called mutual friend Bill Cleary and spoke with him on the phone for more than an hour. Bill didn't know the location either, but he had spoken with Sean after the discovery, and learned that the depth was approximately 190 feet.

Rusty examined his list of hangs. He did not have this list by accident. He had accumulated hang logs over the years, then paid a couple of secretaries $15 per hour to enter the numbers into a database. The result was a searchable database that contained more than 29,000 pairs of hang numbers. The benefit of such a database was that it created groupings, or clusters, of hangs whose multiplicity increased their reliability. Searching clusters saved time and diesel fuel. The list had already proven the value of its investment by enabling him to discover previously unfound shipwrecks: two in one day!

I made a Facebook posting about his double discovery. I titled it:

SHIPWRECK DISCOVERY TWOFER
"Twofer" is a slang word that means "two for one." Thus the title above means "two shipwreck discoveries for one trip."

Not many divers can claim to have discovered two

shipwrecks on a one-day trip. Enter the dive boat RV *Explorer*.

During the summer of 2016, the *Explorer* departed from her dock in Cape May, New Jersey with five people on board: owners and skippers Rusty Cassway and Brian Sullivan, plus divers Stephen Lagreca, Bart Malone, and Tim Terrey. Their destination: to check out deep-water hang numbers offshore of the *India Arrow*.

One might suspect that they were lucky to find even one shipwreck, much less two. Luck had nothing to do with it. It wasn't luck that research unearthed hang numbers; it wasn't luck that forced the team to go diving that day; and it wasn't luck that steered the boat to GPS coordinates of an unknown nature instead of going to a well-known and often-dived shipwreck. It was conscious will and determination that sent these divers to locations that could have proved to be nothing more than a reef, a ledge, or a pile of rocks – as is usually the case with unidentified hang numbers.

The hang-log name of the first set of numbers was Amazing Grace. The name did not necessarily have any meaning. Hangs have been called after the name of the skipper who lost his dredge on the hang, or after the name of a person or persons who were onboard on the day of the incident, or after the name of the boat's mascot: a dog, cat, or canary. This one was named after a scallop boat that disappeared in the vicinity with all hands lost, in 1984. The scalloper's hull was painted maroon; subsequent scallopers found maroon paint on their gear when they hauled in their nets near the hang.

In this case, the wreck that the *Explorer* hooked into on the sandy seafloor actually *was* the *Amazing Grace*. Who would have thought? The depth of the wreck was recorded as 253 feet.

Although the discoverers didn't know it at the time, the loss of the *Amazing Grace* was historically significant as a turning point in the history of safety at sea.

In the 1980's, uninspected fishing vessels were being lost at an alarming rate. As a result, the National Transportation Safety Board charged the U.S. Coast Guard with making recommendations for reducing such losses. Among other items, the single most important factor that the Coast Guard found lacking on fishing vessels was an EPIRB.

EPIRB is the acronym for Emergency Position Indicating Radio Beacon. It is a device that was designed to float off a sinking vessel and to switch itself on upon contact with seawater. The device then transmitted a homing signal on a specific frequency; the transmission directed rescue vessels to the location of the floating EPIRB.

The loss of the *Amazing Grace* and her four-man crew was

the straw that broke the camel's back (to coin a cliché). Legislation was drafted to make EPIRB's required equipment on uninspected vessels, and on vessels that were documented to carry more than six passengers. Thus the loss of the scallop boat's crew was a legacy that has saved countless lives ever since.

Having one feather in their collective cap did not prevent the *Explorer's* skippers and crewmembers from checking out another set of GPS numbers. This time they found and dived on a wreck that proved to be the fishing vessel *Pilgrim's Progress*. The *Pilgrim's Progress* was not as historic as the *Amazing Grace*, and her skipper lived to tell the tale of how she was swamped by a thirty-foot wave. The depth of the *Pilgrim's Progress* was 190 feet.

With regard to the accompanying photos, the *Mabel Susann* is a sister of the *Amazing Grace*, and was built at the same yard. Both photos are courtesy of Rusty Cassway.

The stories of these discoveries, and the histories of these vessels, will be told in much greater detail in a forthcoming book of mine, slated for publication next year. Stay tuned for the announcement.

I published the book in 2018. I called it *Shipwreck Potpourri*. The book was an addendum to my Popular Dive Guide Series. In the book I related stories about newly discovered shipwrecks, newly identified shipwrecks, shipwrecks that for one reason or another had not been

Photo courtesy of Rusty Cassway. He was able to obtain this picture of the *Amazing Grace* after I published the article on Facebook, and after I published the greatly expanded version in *Shipwreck Potpourri*.

It is interesting to note that the National Transportation Safety Board conducted the investigation on the loss of the *Amazing Grace*, and published the Marine Accident Report, instead of the U.S. Coast Guard.

included in the State titles of the Series. It also contained updated information about some shipwrecks that had been included in the Series. The chapter about the *Amazing Grace* and *Pilgrim's Progress* was greatly expanded in order to add more detail than the slender Facebook posting provided.

Rusty's modus operandi was not to rely on single isolated hangs, but to look for clusters where multiple hang numbers created a large footprint instead of a pinpoint. Each pair of numbers consisted of either latitude and longitude, north-south and east-west GPS coordinates, or, in the old days, two lines of loran numbers.

(Loran is the acronym for Long Range Navigation, a triangulating system that is no long in use. The system utilized two time-delay signals that were transmitted from towers whose signal lines ideally lay perpendicular to each other, thus allowing the user to triangulate a position with a fair degree of accuracy.)

The rationale behind clusters was this: each pair of coordinates originated from a boat – generally a dragger or trawler – that hung its net on a target. When a net was hung, the skipper jotted the numbers in a notebook as a reminder to avoid this spot in the future. The numbers did not necessarily refer to the precise location of the hang, but to the position of the boat with respect to the length of the cable that stretched to the target. Each boat would have been travelling in a different direction, so that all the numbers were slightly different, thus creating a cluster of hang numbers around the object that caused the hang. The actual target would generally be near the center of the cluster. The number of hangs indicated that something on the bottom created the hang. Still, in most cases, the hang could be a rock, reef, or ledge instead of a shipwreck.

Rusty searched for hangs along the 190-foot curve on the nautical chart. This search was simultaneously cross referenced to a list of fishing hot spots from another local Cape May charter boat. It did not take long to find a cluster of hangs at a depth of 190 feet in the approximate area in which he thought Sean had found the unknown steamer.

Onboard the *Explorer*, Rusty Cassway and his partner Brian Sullivan, plus Mike Dudas and Tom Packer, departed from Cape May, New Jersey on July 4, 2018. Rusty and his team were in luck – and remember that I use the word "luck" loosely, considering how much time, money, and effort went into creating the hang log database. His calculations or best-guess scenario found the same wreck that Sean had found five days earlier.

As luck would have it – again I use the word "luck" loosely, for luck favors the prepared mind – Rusty found and recovered the ship's brass builder's plaque between the engine and one of the two boilers.

The builder's plaque was not embossed with the name of the vessel, but with the name of the ship builder, the city of construction, and the serial numbers of the engine and boilers. This meant that Rusty had

The tallest structure is the engine. The two cylinders that straddle the engine are the primary boilers; the small cylinder is the donkey boiler. Rusty found the builder's plaque in the surrounding pile of rubble.

© Rustin Cassway 2018

to do some homework in order to identify the wreck. He accomplished in days what would have taken months or years in pre-Internet times. I am envious.

Because the words on the plaque were written in Norwegian, Rusty's first thought was to contact the Norwegian Maritime Museum, in Oslo, Norway. He called the museum on the telephone, but because he could not understand the receptionist's accent, he was unable to obtain the email address of the museum's archivist.

Then he remembered that he had a long-time friend who now lived in Norway: Hildrun Friederike Sommer. To understand this connection, we must go back to 1983. That was the year when 16-year-old Rusty took his scuba diving course from Evelyn Dudas. Evie not only made wetsuits and ran the dive shop, called Dudas Diving Duds, but she also taught scuba courses at night while she was raising four children: Michael, Suzanne, Charlie, and Christine. John Dudas, Evie's husband and partner in the dive shop, had passed away the previous year. Evie hired Rusty to work part time in the shop.

Because Christine was a toddler, she needed more attention than Evie had time to give. So in 1984, she hired Hildrun as her nanny. The dive shop lay only a hundred yards from Dudas' house, so there was a great deal of intermingling as customers and visitors traveled between buildings in search of Evie's current whereabouts. This was how Rusty met Hildrun, and how they become friends.

After his inability to communicate with the receptionist of the Norwegian Maritime Museum, Rusty called Hildrun and asked her to help. She then called the museum in his behalf, and established a connec-

Photo by
Rusty Cassway.

tion with Sven Ahrens, who was in charge of displays in the museum. Hildrun obtained Sven's email address, and relayed the information to Rusty. Via email, Rusty sent to Sven the facts surrounding the shipwreck's discovery and the information on the builder's plaque.

In a trice, figuratively speaking, museum historians found that the number on the plaque correlated with company documentation for a vessel called *Octavian*. The *Octavian* was listed as having been lost with all hands on or about January 17, 1942.

This information was helpful except for one glaring flaw: it contradicted previously accepted dogma about the vessel's loss.

According to the history books, the *Octavian* was torpedoed by the *U-203* on January 17, 1942. But here's the catch: according to those same history books, the *Octavian* was sunk off the coast of Newfoundland, more than a thousand miles from where the wreck actually lay on the seabed.

I accept the theory of continental drift, but seriously doubt that a 1,300-ton sunken freighter could drift as much as an inch, much less hundreds of miles. Continental drift could not be responsible for transporting a fully laden steel hull from Newfoundland to Maryland for another reason: the Newfies would never allow it.

There is also another rub: one that Rusty spotted and pointed out to me, but for some reason the Allied Assessors overlooked. According to the voyage log in the Norwegian Maritime Museum, on the *Octavian's* final passage she was on route from Galveston, Texas to St. John, New Brunswick, Canada. To make such a passage, the *Octavian* would have crossed the Gulf of Mexico, rounded the southern tip of Florida, steamed in a northerly direction along the U.S. eastern seaboard, and ducked into the Bay of Fundy on the way to St. John on the New Brunswick mainland. She would never have rounded Nova Scotia to be torpedoed in the Atlantic Ocean.

It seems as if the Allied Assessors thought that the *Octavian* was bound for St. John's, Newfoundland, in which case she would have proceeded past Nova Scotia to the location at which the *U-203* fired a torpedo at some other vessel. In light of the *Octavian's* actual destination, which lacked the "apostrophe ess," there was no doubt that the *U-203* could not be credited on its record of vessel's sunk with the *Octavian's* tonnage.

The true scenario now begs other questions: at which vessel did the *U-203* fire a torpedo, and did that vessel sink with all hands so that there does not exist a report of her loss? Those questions lie beyond the realm of the present volume.

At this point Rusty contacted me. I told him frankly that I had never heard of the *Octavian* – and I wrote the book on U-boat warfare off the U.S. eastern seaboard: *Track of the Gray Wolf* (1989), which I revised and expanded as *The Fuhrer's U-boats in American Waters* (2006).

In shipwreck research – or any research for that matter – a researcher is only as good as his source materials. If those materials were in error, the researcher must necessarily be misled.

Starting research with the name of a vessel is usually fairly straightforward. I have my own personal library of research volumes. The first one that I pulled off the shelf was *Lloyd's War Losses, the Second World War*, purportedly a chronological listing of every merchant vessel that was lost during the war due to enemy action. I was chagrinned to learn that there was no entry for the *Octavian* on the given date, or any other date.

Next I read through the War Diary of the Eastern Sea Frontier. Again there was no mention of the *Octavian*. Of course, there wouldn't be if she were sunk off the coast of Newfoundland. That location was in Canadian waters called the Northwest Atlantic.

Then I tried *Axis Submarine Successes 1939-1945*, by Jurgen Rohwer. Technically speaking, this was a secondary source, not a primary. But Rohwer was a noted history scholar with a Ph.D, he was the director of the Stuttgart Library of Modern History, in Germany, and he had access to original U-boat records and deck logs. His word was generally taken as gospel, but as we will come to see, U-boat gospel has a penchant for being, well, less than gospel. The dictionary definition of gospel is "something accepted as unquestionably true." In the case of the *Octavian*, the historic location of her loss turned out to be patently false.

Rohwer duly noted that the *U-203* (Kapitanleutnant Rolf Mutzelburg) was given credit for sinking the *Octavian* on January 16, 1942, at 60 degrees west latitude and 45 degrees north longitude. *However,* a footnote stated, "The *Octavian* was reported missing after Jan. 16th in this area." That statement seemed to imply that there was a modicum of a particle of an iota of doubt in Rohwer's mind. I inferred from the footnote that Rohwer was not entirely convinced that the *U-203* earned credit for that particular tonnage sunk. Hmmnn.

Directly under the line that denoted the loss of the *Octavian*, the *U-123* (Kapitanleutnant Reinhard Hardegen) was given credit for sinking the *San Jose* on January 17, 1942. *That* piece of information I knew for certain was wrong, because the *San Jose* sank after colliding with the *Santa Elisa*. There were plenty of surviving witnesses to prove that the collision occurred. *But,* due to dense fog, no one actually witnessed the sinking of the *San Jose.*

This collision occurred east of Atlantic City, New Jersey.

The crew abandoned ship in lifeboats. The *A. L. Kent* rescued six survivors, the *Wellhart* rescued eighteen, and the *Charles L. O'Connor* rescued eleven. When a final toll was taken, it was discovered that the entire thirty-five-man crew of the *San Jose* had been saved. Some suffered from exposure, but because they were located so quickly (within a day), none succumbed to its effects.

Due to a cargo of oil in barrels, the *Santa Elisa* burst into flames at the time of the collision. The crew manned their posts and battled the blaze. She burned so furiously that the fire was not extinguished until sixteen hours later. The vessel suffered so much damage that she was unable to proceed under her own power. She was towed to New York City where eventually she was rebuilt and returned to service.

The collision was no secret to Americans. Local residents and tourists in beachfront hotels watched the fire throughout the night. The collision was well covered in local and national newspapers, where it made front page headlines. There was no doubt that the collision occurred.

In *Shipwrecks of New Jersey: South* (2002), I wrote, "Hardegen claimed to have sunk the *San Jose* by torpedo. But then, he also claimed to have sunk the American tanker *Malay* on January 19, after a running gun battle off North Carolina. The *Malay* limped into Newport News [Virginia] with gaping holes in her hull, and was repaired and returned to service."

I also wrote, "Discrepancies must necessarily occur during the heat of battle, and when events are described from a single point of view. Historians often settle disputes and contradictory claims because they are blessed with the vision of hindsight and have access to written records. In this case there can be no doubt that a collision occurred, and that the *San Jose* sank afterward. [I have dived on the wreck many times.] What is *not* known is exactly when the vessel went down, because her crew had abandoned ship. I suppose one could stretch a point and hypothesize that Hardegen happened across the drifting freighter in the fog, perhaps attracted by the flares, fire, or radio transmissions, then launched a torpedo into the drifting hulk and hastened her demise – but that seems unlikely."

However, in a greater context, this entry about Hardegen sinking the *San Jose* now becomes meaningful, even though the claim or assignation was incorrect.

Next I checked *Hitler's U-boat War* (1996), by Clay Blair. Granted that this was also a secondary source, the two-tome set was more like an encyclopedia, totaling 1,700 pages that covered the entire war. The books were meticulously researched and filled with details that established the length to which Blair went in order to obtain and verify his facts. On a number of occasions, he even cited *Track of the Gray Wolf* (1989), by this author, as one of his sources. But that is neither here nor there.

In *Hitler's U-boat War* I found an obscure footnote that read, "Owing to the vivid and precise description of the sinkings of the two 'unidentified' ships for 8,000 tons in Hardegen's log, Gannon was persuaded to credit them. An American researcher, Edward R. Rumpf, suggests that those two ships could have been the 1,300-ton Norwegian *Octavian* and the 5,300-ton Panamanian *Olympic*, whose loss has been attributed to another U-boat."

The *Olympic* was sunk on January 22, 1942, and was credited to the *U-66* (Kapitanleutnant Ernst Kals), which caught up with the *U-123* off the coast of North Carolina.

I do emails in the morning. After doing some follow-up research pursuant to Rusty's email, I got ready to go mountain biking. I sent a hasty reply to Rusty, telling him about the footnote and that the next place to look for follow-up information was Hardegen's deck log (called KGB in German, for Kriegstagebüch).

After the war, the British sent to Berlin a team of archivists and photographers whose job was to microfilm every page of every deck log that was in Germany's possession. The British kindly made copies of all the microfilm reels for the United States. These reels were kept in the National Archives' new facility in College Park, Maryland, called Archives 2. When I started working on *The Fuhrer's U-boats in American Waters*, I printed paper copies of Hardegen's log for the month of January 1942. I did this because he led Paukenschlag; his was the first U-boat to enter American waters since the First World War.

In my email to Rusty, I offered to scan or photocopy my print-out and send it to him. But I cautioned him that the log was written in German. I had already skimmed through the log (in which vessel names were spelled out so that I could read them if not the surrounding text) but saw no mention of the *Octavian*. Then I went biking.

Silly me. As I was speeding along rugged mountain trails, my wandering mind remembered that later – after I had published *The Fuhrer's U-boats in American Waters*, but research never ends – I had obtained a version of Hardegen's log that had been translated into English.

Uhrzeit	Witterung, Beleuchtung, Sichtigkeit der Luft, Mondschein usw.	Vorkommnisse
08.00 12.00		Qu 5497 CA Qu 5756 CA
		Etmal: 140 sm Gesamt: 40848 sm davon: 124 sm
		St.B. voraus ein Licht. Ran! Nach kurzer Zeit konnte ich einen Frachtdpfr. von etwa 4 000 Brt. ausmachen. 4 Ladeluken, tief beladen. Er führte nur am vorderen Mast Dpfr.-Laterne und verdunkelte Positionslampen. Kurs 13°, Fahrt 11 sm. Leider wird es schon hell. Ich setze mich vor und komme etwas nah. Da scheere ich kurz entschlossen in 600 m Abstand vor seinen Bug, lasse den letzten Heckaal klar machen, komme selbst in den dunklen Horizont und schieße bei Lage
13.01	Qu 5756 CA NW2,0/10,See1-2,Si5sm	90° E- 750 m. 57 sec Laufzeit. Eine sehr heftige Detonation, starke, tiefschwarze Sprengsäule. Treffer Brücke. Der Dpfr. schnitt gleic mit der Fahrt unter. Als die Sprengsäule sich verzog, sahen nur noch die Mastspitzen aus dem Wasser, die kurz darauf versanken. Wassertiefe 45 m. Mit Höchstfahrt nach Osten abgelaufen, da es hell wird und ich am Tage etwas mehr Wasser unter Kiel brauche. Da See ruhig und wolkenlos bleibe ich oben, um schnell Cap Hatteras anzusteuern, da dort gem. F.T. sich der Verkehr bündelt.
14.58		Alarm! Flugboot, Typ "Consolidated".
16.09		Qu 5769 CA
16.51		Alarm! Flugboot.
18.43		
20.00		Qu 5799 CA
20.29		Alarm! Landflgzg.
21.14		
22.11	SW.0/10,See0-1,Si15sm	Alarm! Flugboot.

This is the top part of the page in Hardegen's deck log in which the sinking the *Octavian* is described.

Upon returning from my bike trip, I pulled out my folder on the *U-123*, and there they were: both versions. I went directly to January 17, and this is what I read:

Starboard ahead a light. Go for it! After a short time I can recognize a freighter of Approximately 4000 GRT [Gross Registered Tons]. 4 hatches, heavily loaded. He only shows a lamp on the first mast and darkened position lights. Course 13°, speed 11 knots. Unfortunately dawn is breaking. While overtaking I get a bit too close. On the spur of the moment I cross his bow at a distance of 600 meters, prepare the last stern torpedo and get myself into the dark horizon. Fired stern torpedo. Target angle 90°, distance 750 meters. Running time 57 seconds. A very heavy detonation, strong, dark black smoke plume. Hit bridge. The steamer sinks immediately. As the smoke from the detonation cleared, only the masts were still visible above the water, and shortly thereafter sank. Water depth 45 meters. I depart at maximum speed eastwards because the day is dawning and I need some more water under our keel during the day. Due to calm seas and a cloudless sky I decide to stay on the surface to reach Cape Hatteras fast where according to radio messages the shipping crosses.

The vessel in question could have been the *San Jose*, which was abandoned and drifting and already partially damaged. It could have been, but it wasn't. The reason it wasn't the *San Jose* was the location that was given in Hardegen's log: CA 5756.

During World War 2, the German navy (Kriegsmarine) utilized a grid chart system for simplicity in identifying locations at sea. Except for the polar regions, the entire world was represented by coded squares (or sometimes, rectangles). Each major square was given a two-letter code. This major square was divided into nine two-digit squares, 10 through 90. Each numbered square was subdivided into nine more two-digit squares, 10 through 90. Each of the latter squares was further subdivided into nine single-digit squares. Thus each two-lettered square contained nine squares, which contained nine squares, which contained nine more squares: 729 individually numbered squares in all.

Exceptions of convenience were made to this general rule.

Instead of giving his location in latitude and longitude, a U-boat skipper referred to the grid chart, and gave his position by the lettered grid square, one of the nine two-numbered squares within it, then one of the nine two-numbered zero-ending squares within that, then one of the single-numbered squares which took the place of the final zero.

The lettered grid square off the U.S. eastern seaboard, between Rhode Island and Georgia, was designated as CA. Within CA lay the numbered square in which the above action occurred, 57, which designated the ocean offshore of Delaware, Maryland, and Virginia. Within square 57 lay number 50, and within number 50 lay the smallest square, which had the single digit square that converted the zero in 50 to 6, thus yielding 56.

To recapitulate in different words, within CA, Hardegen located grid square 57, within which he located grid square 50, within which he located grid square 6, so that 50 became 56.

This coded grid system did not lead to pinpoint accuracy, nor was it intended to. But it was close enough to enable U-boat Command to ascertain where every U-boat was located whenever it checked in with headquarters.

As should already be obvious, the place where Hardegen made his attack on January 17, 1942, was nowhere near the site of the collision between the *San Jose* and the *Santa Elisa*. The distance between the two locations was 74 nautical miles. The date was the same but not the location.

The coincidence of the date between the two events seems to have

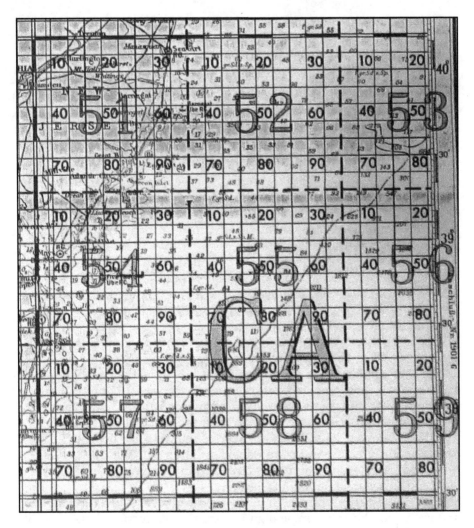

led someone – either the Allied Assessors or Jurgen Rohwer – to conclude that Hardegen had torpedoed the *San Jose*. In any case, that is the way the tonnage credit was given when Rohwer compiled the listings in *Axis Submarine Successes 1939-1945*, subject to his footnote. Perhaps he did not have access to American newspapers, and therefore did not know about the collision. But, there I go speculating again.

In his log, Hardegen did not write the name of the vessel that he sank. The only times he wrote the names of the vessels he attacked were when he intercepted their radio transmissions.

Whenever a vessel transmitted a radio message, the message commenced with the name of the vessel. The name was not spelled out in Morse code, or pronounced in voice communication. Instead, every vessel that was equipped with wireless was assigned a four-letter radio code, much the way in which radio stations are announced. The radio code for the *Octavian* was LJXS. U-boats carried a copy of *Lloyd's Register of Ships*. The *Register* provided each vessel's radio code plus statistical information about the vessel, including her tonnage.

According to Hardegen, who had the vessel in his periscope sight (if the U-boat was under water) or in his binocular lens (if the U-boat was proceeding on the surface with the skipper in the conning tower), the vessel he attacked sank quickly, almost as soon as the smoke cleared from the exploding torpedo.

Neither Hardegen nor any other vessel or land-based radio receiver intercepted a message from the *Octavian*.

From those two facts it is safe to conclude that the *Octavian* did not have time to transmit an SOS; or perhaps the explosion damaged her wireless equipment or its antenna or its wire connection with the antenna.

The *Octavian* sank with all hands, so there were no survivors to report the name of the vessel and her approximate position at the time of her loss.

And so the *Octavian* slipped into anonymity: wrongfully credited to the wrong U-boat and at the wrong location . . .

. . . until Sean Manni discovered her wreckage and Rusty Cassway identified her remains.

The next morning I sent an email to Rusty in which I told him that I had suddenly remembered that I had an English translation of Hardegen's log. Would he like me to send him a scan or photocopy? He replied that he had told Mike Dudas about the log, and that Mike had found an English translation on the Internet. So all three of us were on the same page – quite literally.

I planned to stay home and work on my Poconos trail guide that day. But first I wanted to continue my *Octavian* research with reference to Blair's footnote.

I had never heard of Edward Rumpf. He must have kept a low profile, and must never have published anything on the subject about which Blair thought that he had much information. Not every researcher is an author. I was unable to find any mention of his work on the Internet. The name Edward Rumpf appeared, but not in relation to U-boats.

I was familiar with Michael Gannon because I had a copy of his book, *Operation Drumbeat*, which was published in 1990, one year after *Track of the Gray Wolf* was published.

Gannon noted that in his log, Hardegen claimed to have actually observed the unnamed vessel sink beneath the surface on January 17,

1942. Gannon also noted, "No notice of a missing ship in the geographical vicinity or of a ship's failure to make a port of destination in this general time period is on file in the pertinent archives. Is there a wreck at that position, CA 5756, which corresponds to map coordinates 37-50N, 74-10W?" (In actuality, the coordinates were 38-00 north, 74-21 west.)

How prescient. No such wreck was known at that location at that time, but there is now: the *Octavian*.

This is not to say that every word in Hardegen's log was gospel. Just two days after the *Octavian* incident, on January 19, Hardegen attacked the tanker *Malay* with shells from his deck gun. The *Malay* caught fire but the crew managed to extinguish the flames. The *Malay* escaped under the cover of darkness. Hardegen's pursuit was delayed because he turned away in order to fire a torpedo at another vessel. The *Malay*'s cargo tanks were empty because she was on a return passage; she was able to maintain a speed of 11 knots. Hardegen eventually caught up with her and fired a torpedo that struck amidships. Yet the *Malay* still managed to stay afloat.

The U-boat's radio intercepted the *Malay*'s calls for help, and Hardegen recorded them in the log: "SOS sinking rapidly, next ship please hurry, torpedoed, sinking." and "Hurry, hurry, next ship."

Hardegen then wrote, "Therefore we can count him as completely destroyed."

This statement was premature. The *Malay*'s speed was reduced as a result of the torpedo damage, but she maintained her course and avoided further confrontation. Captain John Dodge, master of the *Malay*, fired flares so that Coast Guard cutters, alerted by wireless and rushing to the scene, could locate the fleeing tanker. One cutter removed the injured men and raced to Norfolk, Virginia where they could receive medical attention.

The *Malay* limped along under armed escort and eventually reached Newport News, Virginia. She went to sea again after $170,000 worth of repairs were made.

My point in relating this action is that a solitary source is not necessarily gospel. Only when that source is compared with other sources and agreement is found, can historians connect the dots in order to arrive at a conclusion that seems the most logical.

While I am on the subject of deck logs in general and Hardegen in particular, with regard to the *San Jose*, in *The Fuhrer's U-boats in American Waters*, I also posed the suggestion, "Perhaps German propaganda claimed the sinking for the purpose of morale. Possibly, Hardegen falsified his log in order to increase his already impressive tonnage record."

Deck log falsifications are not as farfetched as they might sound. The most infamous case on record occurred when Kapitanleutnant Fritz-Julius Lemp of the *U-30* torpedoed and sank the British passenger liner *Athenia* on September 3, 1939. This was the very first U-boat attack of Hitler's war. Germany had invaded Poland only two days previous, thus precipitating World War Two. According to the rules of engagement at that time, U-boats were authorized to attack only British and French warships, not passenger liners that were filled with non-combatants.

U-boats had already been deployed in anticipation of the invasion and the onset of war. They were roaming the Atlantic Ocean awaiting word from U-boat headquarters to commence hostilities. That word was transmitted to Germany's naval fleet at 12:56 p.m. on September 3, 1939. Lemp wasted no time in finding and attacking the first casualty of the war, barely seven hours after the official declaration.

Lemp's fatal error was in mistaking the silhouette of the *Athenia* for that of a British armed cruiser or an armed merchant vessel. On board were 1,103 civilians, of whom 311 were American. Shades of the *Lusitania* from the first world war. At this point, Lemp could have admitted his error and helped to rescue passengers and crew. Instead, he maintained radio silence, and slunk away under water.

The *Athenia* transmitted a call for help: not the SOS of peacetime protocol, but SSS, a signal that meant a U-boat attack. A number of vessels rushed to the aid of the slowly sinking liner, which remained afloat all night before sinking in the morning. Shades of the *Andrea Doria*. Most of the people onboard the *Athenia* were rescued. The casualty rate turned out to be 118 people, of whom 28 were America citizens.

When Lemp returned from patrol, he admitted to Admiral Karl Donitz that he had torpedoed the *Athenia* after misidentifying her. Donitz then ordered Lemp to expunge all mention of the incident from his deck log.

Hitler denied responsibility for the attack. Nazi propaganda blamed the British, claiming that the vessel was sunk by a British mine or submarine, then later went as far as to contend that the British sank the *Athenia* deliberately in order to stir neutral nations into joining the Allies in the war against Nazism. Germany sustained the cover-up throughout the war. The truth was not divulged until after Germany's capitulation.

On June 20, 1941, Hardegen – who had just taken command of the *U-123* – must have been overeager to commence his tonnage count. He torpedoed, shelled, and finally sank the Portuguese vessel *Ganda*. Portugal was a neutral nation and therefore her vessels were not sanctioned targets. This was a serious offense that Hitler did not want known to the world at large. In response to political outrage, he claimed that Germany was innocent and that the *Ganda* must have be sunk by a British submarine.

Once again Donitz passed the order for a deck log erasure. Hardegen duly altered both his deck log and attack report so that neither one revealed his responsibility for the event. Thus my proposition that Hardegen falsified his deck log with regard to the *San Jose* as a distinct possibility . . . but one that turned out to be wrong.

Hardegen clearly was responsible for sinking the *Octavian*. Either the Allied Assessors or Jurgen Rohwer erred in giving him credit for the *San Jose*: an absurd assignation in light of the fact of her collision with the *Santa Elisa*, which not only garnered front page news, but which occurred nearly a hundred miles from the location from which Hardegen fired a torpedo into a target that he watched as she sank beneath the surface of the sea.

This blatant disregard of recorded facts casts doubt on the ability of the Allied Assessors to have made appropriate analyses of U-boat attacks with respect to Allied vessel losses: another case of gospel biting the dust. In this case, the fact that the Allied Assessors did not have access to Ultra decrypts is irrelevant.

It also casts doubt on Jurgen Rohwer's *Axis Submarine Successes 1939-1945* (1968) as he concurred with the Allied Assessors despite the geographical differences and *with* access to Ultra decrypts (after the updated 1983 edition). Yet another case of gospel biting the dust.

At this point I should mention that Rohwer claimed, "The *Esparta*, *Malchace*, and *Tamaulipas* were sunk in shallow water, but were total losses." When I later dived on the *Esparta*, off the coast of Georgia, I was astonished to learn that the depth was only 50 feet. The *Tamaulipas* lay in 155 feet of water, and the *Malchace* in 205 feet. Neither of these depths qualify as shallow. Oh, well.

To return to Gannon's book, *Operation Drumbeat* (1990), and the relevant passages, Gannon did not mention the *Octavian* by name, but what I found there was interesting if inconclusive. First, Gannon concurred with my suggestion in *Track of the Gray Wolf*, which was published the year before *Operation Drumbeat*, that Hardegen was guilty of altering his U-boat deck log. But not for taking credit for sinking the *San Jose* on January 17, 1942.

Gannon called attention to the *Ganda* incident. He then blamed Jurgen Rohwer for giving credit to Hardegen for sinking the *San Jose*, not the Allied Assessors. At this point, let me break the chronological narrative in order to educate my readers about how it came about, in the normal course of events, that U-boat credit assignments were made and compiled.

Ultra Decrypt and Allied Assessors

The most closely guarded secret of World War Two was code-breaking intelligence.

Every U-boat carried an encryption machine called Enigma. Prior to transmission, outgoing messages were encoded by a complicated system of wheels and disks. Incoming messages had to be decoded by Enigma before they could be read.

A porthole on the wreck of the *Malchace*.

Polish and British mathematicians broke the German machine ciphers early in the war. For some time afterward, Britain did not let anyone – including the U.S. – know that it was reading German transmissions. British radios monitored transmissions from U-boat Control to the various U-boats at sea, as well as transmissions from individual U-boats to U-boat Control.

These messages were forwarded to code breakers at Bletchley Park, in London. Intelligence experts deciphered the messages, collated the information, and wrote analyses for use by military authorities, none of whom knew where the intelligence originated. Decoded messages were dispatched to appropriate commands. These decoded messages, or decrypts, were stamped Ultra Top Secret (which meant above and beyond Top Secret). Thus the British were able to read operational orders, U-boat movements, attack reports, and so on.

Communiqués between Doenitz and his wolf packs not only offered insights into the way in which the Admiral was running the U-boat war, but they provided the exact location of any U-boat that transmitted its position to U-boat Control. In addition, high-frequency direction-finding technology (known as HF/DF, pronounced huff-duff) was used to obtain radio fixes on a U-boat's transmission location.

The position of every U-boat was plotted on a gigantic plotting board. Constant updates permitted staff officers to note each U-boat's current position, to track its course, and to project its track by extrapolating its speed and bearing.

After the U.S. entered the war, the Brits shared this information

The Secret Room of the Eastern Sea Frontier. Note the large-scale chart on the wall to the right, where a man and a woman are logging positions off North Carolina.

with U.S. Naval intelligence experts. The Navy established a Submarine Tracking Room in Washington, DC; it was the American counterpart of the British facility at Bletchley Park.

Eventually, there grew a need for greater organization and dissemination of Ultra decrypts. In May 1943, the U.S. Navy created a separate antisubmarine command that was known as the Tenth Fleet. The Tenth Fleet was staffed by some fifty personnel, but had no ships.

Adjacent to the Submarine Tracking Room was a "Secret Room." This room was kept locked at all times. Only five people had keys to this room: the lieutenant in charge (John Parsons), his assistant John Boland, two yeomen, and "the Navy's principal U-boat tracker, Kenneth Knowles." The Secret Room was where all the U-boats' positions were plotted from Ultra decrypts. Commander Knowles then transferred these positions to the Submarine Tracking Room "without revealing the source of his information."

A Submarine Tracking Officer was assigned to make course interpolations that were based not only on enemy transmissions, but on reported sightings. In the plotting room, the STO drew tracks on a huge wall chart. These tracks were updated continuously as new intelligence was received or intercepted. This system enabled the STO to extrapolate the time at which a particular U-boat might arrive at a specified location. He would then disseminate this information to Navy hunter-killer groups that consisted of small aircraft carriers and heavily armed escorts. These hunter-killer groups would crisscross the predicted coordinates, and pounce on the unwary U-boat with a multitude of planes and fast escort vessels that dropped depth charges and hedgehogs with incredible accuracy. It was this awesome offensive power that eventually placed U-boats on the defensive.

After Germany's capitulation, the Allies organized an Assessment Committee that was charged with the monumental task of culling German U-boat records for the purpose of determining which U-boats were responsible for sinking which Allied vessels, and which warships and aircraft should be given credit for sinking which U-boats.

But, the Assessment Committee was not given access to Ultra.

As noted above, the breaking of the German codes was the most closely guarded secret of the war - and it remained the most closely guarded secret until thirty years *after* the war. In the United States, the Official Secrets Act included provisions for severe penalties for anyone who released information about Ultra decryption.

Only twenty years had passed between the end of the Kaiser's bid for world domination, and the commencement of the Fuhrer's bid to conquer the world. To the average person, it might appear that the cultural imperative of the German people was aberrant: Germans either lacked good conscience or were pathologically unstable. Twice in the span of a single generation, they had been led like sheep to follow brutal and bloodthirsty leaders who convinced them that they had the right to enslave the rest of humanity. Some people were understandably nervous about another display of German might.

If Germany learned that its codes had been broken, it could be presumed that it would develop a new encryption system in contemplation of another war. As long as Germany was secure in the wrongful knowledge that its encryption system was secure, it would lack the incentive to develop a new and more complex system.

But the real reason for secrecy was far more prescient: the U.S. and England did not trust their temporary ally, and were already anticipating trouble with Russia after the war. The Soviets were unaware of the code-breaking success and Ultra decrypts. Whenever U.S. and British intelligence units forwarded information to their Russian counterparts, the originating source was withheld. This led Russia to believe that the information originated from spies. Russia was primarily concerned with the accuracy of intelligence, not its origin. As long as the Soviets believed that human informers were responsible for intelligence leaks, and accepted the ability of the U.S. and England to plant spies and recruit local agents, their natural paranoia would induce them to look for spies that did not exist. This would cause them to waste precious time and energy in a worthless pursuit, while protecting the secret that gave the Allies a military advantage in gathering intelligence.

The Assessment Committee based its assessments on partial information. By extrapolation, every assessment that the Committee made is suspect. I make this statement without prejudice. The vogue today is to bash the Allied Assessors for making the errors that they made. On the contrary, I think they did a remarkable job in consideration of the fact that so much of the truth was withheld from them. By way of comparison, if you were asked to tabulate a column of numbers in an arithmetic test, and were not given all the numbers, how close do you think you could get to the correct sum?

In England, everyone who worked at Bletchley Park, or who possessed privileged knowledge of Enigma decryption, was prevented by law from releasing information about decoding operations for *fifty* years. Despite this extra security measure, the Ultra secret was exposed when it became publicly available in the U.S. in 1975, because in accordance with U.S. law, official secrets were protected for only *thirty* years.

By then, evaluations of the U-boat war were firmly implanted in the historical record. The circumstances surrounding U-boat losses and successes were cast in a substance that was longer lasting than bronze: they were cast in ink. The flaws that were inherent in the assessment system persevered. Allied Assessments became gospel.

There's that word again: gospel.

I have often said that a researcher is only as good as his source materials. If those source materials are flawed, the researcher is led down a lane that leads to wrong conclusions.

Another instance that concerns Hardegen and false reports pertains to the *Aurania*, a 13,984-ton British ocean liner that was converted to an armed merchant cruiser by being fitted with deck guns and by carrying a large naval gun crew.

On October 21, 1941, Hardegen fired a torpedo that struck the cruiser's hull soundly. As the vessel slowly flooded, the skipper ordered the lifeboats swung out on their davits in preparation for abandoning ship. One lifeboat was actually launched by six overzealous crewmen. The lifeboat capsized while the *Aurania* was escaping at 8 knots.

Hardegen was forced to submerge when the British destroyers *Croome* and *Totland* sped to attack the U-boat. A slew of depth charges rained down on the *U-123*. When the sea was clear to surface, Hardegen chased the vessels in hopes of sinking another one of the convoy, but the convoy outdistanced him. He then returned to the site of the attack against the *Aurania*. The armed merchant cruiser was nowhere in sight, but he found a capsized lifeboat to which a lone sailor was clinging.

Hardegen rescued the survivor, who gave his name as Bertie Shaw. Under interrogation, Shaw claimed that the *Aurania* had sunk. He told this lie so that Hardegen would not continue his pursuit of the damaged cruiser/liner. Hardegen radioed to U-boat headquarters that he had sunk the *Aurania*, and claimed the tonnage for his record.

In fact, the *Aurania* limped into safe harbor. She was repaired and returned to service for the remainder of the war.

Nonetheless, German records and *Axis Submarine Successes 1939-1945* gave official credit to Hardegen for the largest vessel that he supposedly sank. Thus Hardegen's tonnage total is nowhere near correct the way it was accepted by U-boat command and published after the war.

U-boat records are rife with mistakes and numerous conflicting accounts, mostly due to the confusion under which the U-boat war was fought.

Revision

In order to set the record straight – about ships that were sunk by enemy action in the Eastern Sea Frontier during World War Two – I will take this opportunity to update Appendix 4 from *The Fuhrer's U-boats in American Waters*. That appendix was named Vessel Losses and Fatalities. It consisted of the cumulative statistics with regard the amount of tonnage that was sunk, the number of survivors from vessels that were attacked, and the number of fatalities from the vessels that were attacked.

Year/Month	Totals Tonnage	Survivors	Fatalities
1942 January	95,345	311	596
1942 February	88,789	327	403
1942 March	161,010	745	546
1942 April	147,615	1,369	307
1942 May	22,019	121	49
1942 June	78,397	1,004	182
1942 July	17,618	202	14
Sub-totals	610,793	4,079	2,097
1943	35,351	249	178
1944	16,475	58	68
1945	21,227	139	68
Sub-totals	73,053	446	314
Grand totals	684,846	4,525	2,411

120 vessels sunk (of which parts of two were salvaged)

To the grand totals must be added the following:
The *Octavian* was sunk on January 17, 1942.
The *Miraflores* was sunk on February 19, 1942.

Here are the revised statistics:

Year/Month	Tonnage	Survivors	Fatalities
1942 January	1,335		17
1942 February	2,158		28
Subtotals	614,286		2,142
Grand totals	688,339		2,456

122 vessels sunk (of which parts of two were salvaged)

The ultimate chapter in the American U-boat campaign has yet to be written with finality.

Back to the Narrative

I did not know the location of the wreck. But Rusty did. When he compared the attack location in Hardegen's deck log with the GPS numbers of the wreck of the *Octavian*, he found that the locations differed by only 800 yards: barely half a mile! Hardegen's description of the vessel as a freighter also matches the *Octavian*.

Thus in one fell swoop, Rusty not only identified the shipwreck, but he corrected the history books about which U-boat was responsible for sinking the *Octavian*, and where it was sunk. And he did all this in less than a week. I reek with envy.

But that's not the end of the story. Rusty has cleaned and preserved the builder's plaque, and has made arrangements with the Norwegian Maritime Museum to travel to Norway in order to donate the plaque for display in the museum.

The plaque presentation was scheduled for May 8th, 2019, Norway's day of liberation from Germany in 1945. More than 40 families of *Octavian* victims have been contacted and will be invited to this presentation, thus connecting "those who seek" with families who have questioned what happened to their brave seafaring relatives who disappeared on January 17, 1942. Now they have the answers.

The individual who was responsible for taking the lives of the *Octavian*'s crew was Reinhard Hardegen.

Left: Hardegen's official portrait.

Right: Hardegen wearing the Iron Cross, which he received for the number of his "kills."

(Both from the author's collection.)

C4 - U-boats Against the Americas

In all of mankind's presence on Earth, the two most earthshaking events have been started by men who were born poor.

The first one was good, some say blessed. The second one was bad, some say evil.

The first one was a Jew. The second one hated Jews with a passion that was psychopathic.

The first one has come to be loved by more people than any other person who ever lived. The second one has come to be hated just as much and by as many as the first one is loved.

The first one was Jesus Christ. The second one was Adolf Hitler.

These two influential men have shaped human cultural evolution in ways that were diametrically opposed.

The first one defied the ruling class and became deified. The second one confronted all the nations and became vilified.

These adversarial approaches to life might lead one to wonder what drives a person to threaten his life by challenging the status quo. The current state of affairs notwithstanding, both these men went against the grain knowingly: the first one with no hope of winning, the second one with megalomaniacal perseverance that he could overcome all odds and dominate the world.

The irony of these analogous but contrary individuals is that the first one achieved the goal that he preached, albeit posthumously, while the second one failed badly and committed suicide. Both will be remembered for as long as mankind exists.

There is no need to write a history of the first one. His deeds were well covered in the *New Testament* of the *Holy Bible*.

Likewise, numerous books have been written about the second one. I need not repeat what is now common knowledge.

For the subject of the present book, all we need to know about Hitler is that he initiated the construction of Unterseeboots – naval submarines that are called U-boats in English – in anticipation of using them against vessels of foreign nationalities that would unite against him and against his quest for world domination.

The person Hitler chose to lead his Kriegsmarine (the U-boat arm of Nazi Germany's navy) was Gross Admiral Karl Dönitz (in German, or Doenitz in English, which lacks the umlaut that affects the pronunciation of a vowel that is topped by

My grandfather was a deacon in the Baptist church. He gave this New Testament to me when I was 8 years old. It took me a while but eventually I read every word.

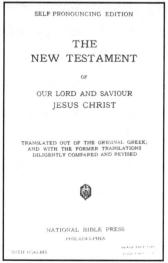

SELF PRONOUNCING EDITION

THE
NEW TESTAMENT

OF

OUR LORD AND SAVIOUR
JESUS CHRIST

TRANSLATED OUT OF THE ORIGINAL GREEK;
AND WITH THE FORMER TRANSLATIONS
DILIGENTLY COMPARED AND REVISED

NATIONAL BIBLE PRESS
PHILADELPHIA

WITH PSALMS

Adolf Hitler was such a megalomaniac that he had his likeness placed on German postage stamps.

an umlaut). Doenitz served in the Kaiser's fledgling U-boat arm during World War One. He started as a watch officer, and quickly rose through the ranks so that near war's end he was given his own command: the *UC-25*. (The "UC" designation referred to a mine-laying U-boat.)

In the middle of 1918, he was transferred to command the *UB-68*: a small coastal U-boat with limited range due to its small size, which translated to reduced fuel capacity and restricted space for the stowage of food for the crew. His theater of operations was the Mediterranean Sea. After only three months at sea, machinery breakdowns forced him to surface. With British warships closing in on him, Doenitz ordered the U-boat scuttled so that it would not fall into enemy hands. He and the entire crew were captured, and spent the remainder of the war as prisoners.

After the Kaiser's unconditional surrender, the Treaty of Versailles limited the size of warships and the aggregate tonnage that the German navy was allowed to maintain. In addition, Germany was stripped of its U-boats and was not permitted to build or buy any replacements. Ever. This firm resolve against U-boats was due to the insistence of perhaps the greatest statesman who ever lived, Prime Minister Winston Churchill, who viewed U-boats as a most deadly weapon that was an underhanded and dangerous threat to worldwide peace. Thus U-boats were banned in the same way in which mustard gas was banned.

Perchance in a moment of mockery, Churchill distinguished U-boats from Allied submarines thus: "Enemy submarines are to be called U-boats. The term submarine is to be reserved for Allied underwater vessels. U-boats are those dastardly villains who sink our ships, while submarines are those gallant and noble craft which sink theirs."

Churchill never lost his warranted fear of U-boats. His dread of their capacity to cripple Allied shipping carried over into Germany's second bid for world domination. He wrote, "The only thing that ever really frightened me during the war was the U-boat peril." He was one of the few who recognized the U-boat as a definite danger to merchant vessels that transported the much needed food, supplies, and materiel that England needed to support the war against the Nazis.

The person who agreed with Churchill the most was Karl Doenitz. He remained in the navy throughout the peacetime years, and continued to rise through the ranks of Germany's small and inadequate navy. In reality, Germany did not need a large navy – or any navy at all – because the world was at peace, and no bordering nation exhibited ambitions to attack or invade Germany. But once the Nazi's took over the country, Hitler started shouting about Lebensraum: German for "living space," and defined in the dictionary as "additional territory deemed necessary to a nation for its economic well-being."

The Nazis used Lebensraum as an excuse to contemplate the takeover of adjacent countries that were militarily weaker than Germany. Toward this end, the Nazis pushed to renegotiate the Treaty of Versailles. The result was the 1935 Anglo-German Naval Agreement, which allowed Germany to increase the size of its capital ships and to enlarge the aggregate tonnage of its navy. This Agreement was followed in 1936 by the Second London Submarine Agreement. Like the first London Submarine Agreement of 1930, and the prior Washington Naval Agreement, this latest version of naval armament limitation further refined the size of warships and the aggregate tonnage of navies, but it also allowed Germany to possess a small number of U-boats.

At this time Churchill was no longer Prime Minister; nor did he hold any position in the British government, else undoubtedly he would have fiercely disagreed with this latter ease in U-boat regulations.

The person who was the most ecstatic about the easing of the Treaty of Versailles was Karl Doenitz. Doenitz joined the German navy in 1913, at the age of 21. As an ensign he first served on the cruiser *Breslau*. The onset of the Great War (1914) found the *Breslau* and the battleship *Goeben* in the Mediterranean Sea. Both ships made a dramatic escape to Constantinople (known previously as Byzantium, now called Istanbul), Turkey. Duty on the Black Sea was lackluster at best, so Doenitz applied for a transfer to the fledgling U-boat service.

Karl Doenitz as a young officer. (From the author's collection.)

As already noted, Doenitz was promoted to Oberleutnant and given command of the *U-25*. Subsequently he took command of the *U-68*. In 1918, as the war was winding down and stood only a month away from Germany's capitulation, he attacked an Allied convoy off the coast of the Republic of Malta, in the Mediterranean Sea. Both a British armed trawler and an armed steamship returned the attack, the former with depth charges and the latter with gunfire. The U-boat was damaged beyond immediate repair. The *U-68* surfaced under fire. Doenitz issued orders to scuttle the boat. After the U-boat slipped beneath the waves, Doenitz and his crew were rescued by the British warship, whereupon they were sent to a prisoner of-war camp.

After his release, Doenitz was convinced to remain in the miniscule navy that Germany was allowed to possess. There was not much for him to do during the following decade. Germany had neither capital ships nor U-boats. Navy personnel merely went through the motions of maintaining their post-war status under the lagging Weimar regime.

Doenitz joined the up-and-coming Nazi party in 1930. He thought that the aggressive political group would eventually violate the terms of the Treaty of Versailles, and commence to rebuild the fleet. He was right. At first, Nazi Germany worked in secret by building aircraft and auxiliary vessels that were hidden from the eyes of Allied examiners who enforced the restrictions of the treaty.

Additionally, the Nazis had U-boat hull sections and interior components manufactured in widespread locations across the country, where the examiners would not think to look. These various parts could then be transported clandestinely to a shipyard where they could be assembled in very short order.

In 1935, Hitler negotiated some easements in the treaty restrictions against a German navy. This allowed Germany to possess a small fleet of warships. He started an aggressive construction program that far exceeded the allowable size of warships and the allowable size of the fleet.

Finally, in 1936, Hitler openly disavowed the Treaty of Versailles and its restrictions against Germany's production of all military arms and ammunition. The Allied nations could do nothing about it but wage war. Hitler ignored all threats.

The Nazis then commenced an unlimited manufacturing undertaking in which they built from scratch a large naval fleet of destroyers, cruisers, battleships, and U-boats; an air force of bombers and fighter planes; an arsenal of artillery, armored vehicles, and tanks; and they started to experiment with long-range ballistic missiles which later rained down on London.

Hitler was gearing for war.

Meanwhile, Doenitz developed tactics for utilizing U-boats to their best advantage, instead of adhering to the International Agreement which stipulated rules for the way in which submarines could engage in warfare. At that time, undersea craft had to abide by "cruiser rules." Doenitz described his understanding of the Agreement like this: "The U-boat was required to act in the same manner as a surface vessel;

whether the merchant ship were armed or not, the U-boat had to surface before it could halt and examine it. If, under the conditions of the
Prize Ordinance with regard to nationality and/or cargo, the U-boat
was entitled to sink the vessel, it was first required to ensure the safety
of the crew; on the high seas the lifeboats carried by the merchant vessel were not deemed to be adequate for the purpose.

"Under the Prize Ordinance the U-boat was exempted from these
obligations of prior examination in the case of:

"1. Merchantmen proceeding under escort of enemy warships or
aircraft.

"2. Merchant vessels which take part in any engagement or which
resist when called up to submit to inspection.

"3. Transports, which are deemed to be on active service, to belong
to the armed forces, and are therefore to be regarded as warships."

The acquisition of U-boats was slow in coming. Admiral Erich
Raeder, Commander-in-Chief of the German navy, did not share Doenitz's enthusiasm for U-boats. Raeder focused on building large capital
ships, and expressed disdain for U-boats. By 1938, the German navy
possessed only a handful of U-boats, with more coming slowly off the
ways. In what almost seems like a demotion, in January of 1939, Doenitz was promoted to Commodore and given command of the navy's
tiny fleet of U-boats.

In his new position, and with war in Europe obviously on the horizon (at least, in the minds of Hitler and the newly elected British Prime
Minister, Winston Churchill), Doenitz was able to divert more naval
funding for the Nazi U-boat arm. So it was that when the German army
invaded Poland – on September 1, 1939 – and two days later both England and France declared war on Germany, Doenitz had managed to
have nearly five dozen U-boats in active operation, with trained crews
ready to take them to sea and engage the enemies that Hitler had
created.

Doenitz was promoted to Rear Admiral a month later. His U-boats
were practically unopposed at sea. This situation arose partly because
the Allies were unaware that Germany had secretly expanded its U-
boat production to such a high degree. The Allies were therefore un-
prepared to meet the demands that were imposed upon its fleet of
warships.

In the first five months of the war, Doenitz's U-boats sank nearly
two hundred vessels, most of them merchant vessels that were keeping
the British people fed and both England and France armed. As a direct
consequence of these U-boat victories, Doenitz was promoted to Vice
Admiral.

This latest promotion, along with the U-boats' phenomenal success
at sea, gave Doenitz a far greater voice in obtaining funding to increase
the size of the U-boat fleet. U-boat construction went into high gear,
and stayed in high gear for the remainder of the war. U-boat sailors

called these early years in the war the "happy time," because the proportion of successful attacks against Allied shipping, when compared to U-boat losses, was extraordinarily high on the side of success.

This situation was due in large part to Doenitz's abnegation of cruiser rules. He ordered his submariners to attack any and all high-seas vessels that were not registered to neutral nations. This order ignored the difficulty of making such a determination at night or in fog when visibility prevented U-boat skippers from observing nationality flags that neutral vessels flew.

The swastika on the flag clearly shows that the U-boat arm of the German navy was fighting for the Nazi government.

Doenitz also ordered his skippers not to render aid to survivors. This ruthless operational procedure resulted in the suffering and death of thousands of merchant mariners.

Doenitz further initiated a system that he called "rudeltaktik." The literal translation of rudeltaktik is "pack tactics," but in idiomatic English it came to be called "wolf pack tactics."

This coordinated attack plan was designed to be employed against convoys, not individual vessels. In its most basic form, whenever a U-boat sighted a convoy, instead of attacking individually, the skipper alerted U-boat headquarters by radio, and gave the position and heading of the convoy. Doenitz then notified all U-boats in the area to proceed to the convoy's projected position, surround the convoy, then wait for the order to attack. Once all the available U-boats were in position, they were ordered to attack at the same time from different directions.

In this manner the escorts were thrown into a rout. Instead of concentrating a number of defenders against a lone U-boat, the escorts were forced to fight singly on multiple fronts. This weakened defense not only enabled the U-boats to escape destruction, but it also allowed some of them to make additional attacks against the now undefended merchant vessels.

Surreptitiously succoring the beleaguered Allied forces was the United States of America. Technically, the U.S. was a neutral nation, because she had not declared war against Nazi Germany. Initially there were perturbations among the American populace about which side the country should join. Although this dichotomy may come as a shock to today's general populace, there was some justification for siding with Germany, because England had placed a blockade around German ports.

Some Americans, shipping companies especially, felt that the blockade restricted free trade, which it undeniably did. The war against the loss of free trade goes back to the American Civil War, when the Union blockaded Confederate ports, which restricted England's commerce with the Southern States. The difference was that now the roles were reversed. The United States felt justified to enforce a blockade when it was to its advantage to do so. Now that same United States objected to a blockade that prevented its free trade.

In reality, however, most of those in power leaned more toward siding with the Allies than with the Nazis. This attitude dominated because Nazi Germany was bent on world domination, whereas the Allies were fighting to uphold the freedom of sovereign nations. While the United States presented an image of neutrality to the world, that image was little more than a façade.

Lend-Lease

President Franklin Delano Roosevelt established secret negotiations with England to produce ways in which the United States could secretly aid England without sending troops, which would have been a clear violation of international law. The policy that evolved from political discussions between the two nations was termed Lend-Lease.

In short, Lend-Lease was a program in which the United States agreed to "lend" fifty aged Navy destroyers and ten old Coast Guard cutters to the British navy, in exchange for "leases" for military bases on British soil. The phrase "British soil" did not limit land acquisitions to the home islands, but extended to British possessions around the world.

In addition, the United States merchant fleet was used to transport much-needed food, arms, and munitions to the beleaguered British homeland from American farmers and manufacturers, who were paid for their meat, produce, and products by the federal government, until such time as England was in a financial position to repay Uncle Sam.

This program implied that there was little or no doubt about whose side the United States was backing in the war to end all wars.

The Day of Infamy

Billy Mitchell was an American fighter pilot who flew with the British in World War One while the fledgling American flying corps was gathering its wits on home soil. After the Army sent planes and pilots to the fighting front in France, Mitchell took command of the Army Air Corps and led it to victory over the Kaiser's aerial squadrons. He returned to the United States as a full bird colonel, and was soon promoted to Brigadier General.

Mitchell was so outspoken about the success of aerial combat as both a defensive and an offensive force that he was called a fanatic by those who opposed his views about the strategic advantage of a strong air force. Nonetheless, he continued to advocate for a separate air force instead of one that was subservient to the Army and Navy.

Furthermore, he professed that aircraft could defeat warships by dropping bombs on the ponderous and slow-moving vessels. To prove his point, he conceived of a test in which his fleet of bombers would attack and sink not only small naval vessels such as U-boats and destroyers, but could even sink cruisers and battleships. The Navy stood its ground (or water), claiming that it was impossible for his mosquito fleet to sink such a well-armored and compartmented hull of which battleships were constructed.

The Navy did everything it could do to stymy Mitchell's plans: it appealed directly to Washington that the general was a madman, that the country needed a stronger Navy and had no allocations for a useless air force, that planes could have no effect against thickly armored warships.

Mitchell had enough political influence to make his dream attack come true. After Germany's unconditional surrender, the belligerent nation was stripped of its navy. In particular, then Prime Minister Winston Churchill demanded fervently that all German U-boats be either scuttled or taken over by Allied countries for examination and testing purposes, and then be either scrapped or scuttled in water so deep that they could not be salvaged. The final date of destruction was August 9, 1921.

The United States Navy acquired eleven German warships: six U-boats (*U-111*, *U-117*, *U-140*, *UB-88*, *UB-148*, and *UC-97*), three destroyers (*G-102*, *S-132*, and *V-43*), the cruiser *Frankfurt*, and the battleship *Ostfriesland*.

With regard to the U-boats, the Navy's initial findings indicated that:

"(a) The Diesel engines of these submarines are superior to any other Diesel engines in any other submarines in commission in the world.

"(b) The periscopes are equal, if not superior, to any other periscope.

"(c) The radius of action of these boats, type for type, is greater than that obtained by other nations.

"(d) Their double hull method of construction is probably superior to other types of construction, so far as protection against depth bombs is concerned."

As a result of these observations, German materials and construction methods were then incorporated into the construction of United States Navy vessels, U-boats especially. The engines of several Ameri-

The ex-German U-boat *U-117* flying the American flag. (Courtesy of the Naval Photographic Center.)

can submarines were redesigned using U-boat engines as models.

When the Navy lost the battle to prevent Mitchell from gaining support for his bombing experiments, it tried to have the target ships placed so far offshore that Mitchell's airplanes would be forced to operate at the extreme limit of their range. The fuel capacity of early biplanes was not great. When Mitchell got wind of this last-gasp sabotage, he put pressure in the proper places and got the ships moved closer to shore. The orders that were finally issued called for all the German warships to be sunk "beyond the fifty fathom curve" (300 feet).

Eight ships were scuttled by naval gunnery or aerial bombing off the coast of Virginia in an area that the Navy designated as the Southern Drill Grounds: *U-117*, *U-140*, *UB-148*, *G-102*, *S-132*, *V-43*, *Frankfurt*, and *Ostfriesland*. The other three U-boats were scuttled elsewhere at various times.

At that time, a depth of three hundred feet was considered beyond human endurance and technical capability.

The scuttling tests of the German warships commenced on June 22, 1921. Mitchell was allowed to bomb only one of the three U-boats (*U-117*); the others were reserved for naval gunfire. He was then permitted to sink only one of the three destroyers (*G-102*); again, the other two were reserved for naval gunfire. It was just as important for the Navy to test the penetration and explosive power of its guns as it was for Mitchell to test his bombs; more so, in

A direct hit on the *U-117*. (From the collection of Hank Keatts.)

the collective mind of the Navy.

Both capital ships were reserved for Mitchell. The protocol for the cruiser *Frankfurt* called for Mitchell's bombers to pound the deck with small bombs first, after which Naval observers boarded the warship in order to inspect the damage that the 100-pound bombs had on German steel. The bombers then dropped 250-pound bombs; again the observers inspected the ship in order to ascertain the extent of the damage. The bombing recommenced with 300-pound bombs.

The observers found that these bombs were unable to penetrate the upper decks. Goats and other animals, which were stationed topside to simulate human crews, were found dead and their bodies mutilated. But the hull and most of the decks were still intact.

Navy inspectors, smugly deciding that aerial bombs alone could never sink the cruiser, ordered the *North Dakota* (BB-29) to prepare time bombs for the final scuttling.

Then came Mitchell's Armageddon with 600-pounders that were dropped by heavy Martin bombers. Bombs rained down so fast and furiously that the *Frankfurt* was immediately shrouded in spray. Tons of sea water fell upon the decks. Crews on the observation ships ran for cover as steel fragments ripped across the water for more than a mile. Before the attack could be called off, so that observers could board and make damage assessments, the *Frankfurt* slipped beneath the waves. Photographic planes recorded with a vengeance the events of July 18.

The ultimate test was yet to come. The *Ostfriesland* was protected by twelve inches of the best armor plate that the German manufacturer Krupp could provide. The hull consisted of four skins for protection against mines and torpedoes. The interior was divided into so many watertight compart-ments that the bat-tleship was thought impregnable, and impossible to sink. At the Battle of Jut-land, the *Ostfries-land* survived a mine explosion and eight-een hits from large gun shells. The bat-tleship was a float-ing fortress of arms and armament.

S. M. Linienschiff „Ostfriesland"

On July 20, the Navy transport *Hen-*derson was packed to the gunwales with over three hundred distinguished guests. In addition to some fifty reporters, there were eight Senators, twelve Congressmen, three Cabinet members (the Secretaries of War, Navy, and Agriculture), and foreign dignitaries from England, France, Spain, Portugal, Brazil, and Japan. The battleship *Pennsylvania* (BB-38) was loaded with admirals, generals, and other high-ranking military officers.

The day dawned miserably, with thirty knot winds whipping the sea to froth. Mitchell and his flyboys sat idly at Langley Field, awaiting the call to strike. When nothing was heard by 1300, Mitchell jumped into his Osprey and flew out to sea. The Navy wanted to call off the attack because of weather – as if battles at sea were always called off due to inclement conditions. Mitchell insisted that the bombing raid be carried out as planned, stating that his planes could fly under those conditions if Navy personnel could observe under them. He went so far as to order his planes into the air without Navy approval.

The Navy was astounded by his impudence, but allowed the attack to proceed. Unfortunately, 250-pound bombs did little damage to the *Ostfriesland's* steel hide. Mitchell's planes landed in a blinding rain storm as reporters raced for shore aboard the *Leary* (DD-158) to report that the battleship was "absolutely intact and undamaged." Many seasick VIP's also returned to shore, convinced that the planes had lost the day.

Mitchell was not to be dissuaded from his convictions. The next morning found him preparing his planes with blockbuster 2,000-pounders. At first he was allowed to drop only 1,000-pounders. Two scored direct hits, and the Navy called off the rest of the attack so they could send observers on board. The found the *Ostfriesland* so badly torn up that they were unable to go below the third deck. They peered through gaping bomb holes at water seeping into the hull below decks.

Then came the big bombs. One by one, seven Martin and Handley-Page bombers made their drops, aiming for near misses, and timing their flights so that each tremendous waterspout settled before the next plane came in for its attack. The concussion of exploding bombs was so severe that observation ships shook when the shock waves reached them. Planes at an altitude of 3,000 feet rocked violently. Thousands of tons of water descended upon the *Ostfriesland's* tattered decks.

The third bomb scored a direct hit on the forecastle; it tore out a frightful hole in the steel hull, and created a raging fire. Another near miss lifted the battleship visibly out of the water. Bomb number five fell near the stern. The *Ostfriesland* began settling aft. When the sixth bomb struck, the after two turrets were already under water. The battleship's bow nosed upward, the ship rolled over onto her port side, and disappeared from view. A Handley-Page delivered the final stroke by dropping the last bomb on the huge vortex of escaping air.

The *Ostfriesland* was gone in a flurry of bubbles.

In keeping with the theme of this book, the reader should know that in 1990, Ken Clayton and this author commenced a multi-year project to locate the eight German warships that were scuttled in the Southern

Although the *Ostfriesland* takes a direct hit in this photograph, near misses were just as effective if not worse in producing damage, because the underwater concussion pummelled hull plates and loosened rivets, which caused flooding. (From the author's collection.)

After Crippling and disabling personnel and armament, heavy bombardment was begun to demonstrate that it was possible to sink Battleships by Air Craft.

Drill Grounds. Over the course of six years, we discovered and dived on seven of the eight. One of the cruisers eluded us.

Although Mitchell was ecstatic about the triumph of his bombers, the Navy refused to accept the implications of his success. The Navy continued to repudiate the general's allegations that a strong and separate air force would change the tide of future warfare. Mitchell refused to renounce his sincerity. Because of his entrenchment, he was railroaded out of the country on foreign assignments that were intended to lose him in red tape and obscurity.

Eventually, as he maintained his verbal attack against Navy obstinancy, by using the press as his sounding board, and by writing articles in popular magazines, he was charged with subversion, and was court-martialed.

Mitchell was in nationwide headline for months. His 1925 trial was the news of the decade. In a military kangaroo court, the outspoken general was found guilty, and was "suspended from rank. command and duty with the forfeiture of all pay and allowances for five years."

This censure did not prevent Mitchell's predictions from coming true. As early as 1923, after he had been mothballed to Hawaii to write a report that no one bothered to read, he forecast the buildup of Japanese air power, and outlined in detail exactly how the Japanese would attack Pearl Harbor and Clark Field: on a Sunday morning when most Navy men would be sleeping late or getting ready for church or spending time with their families.

On Sunday, December 7, 1941, the attack was perpetrated exactly as he stated in his report – a report that had been pigeonholed by military minds that were not prepared to face American vulnerability.

The Honorable G. Katsuda, member of the Japanese House of Peers of Tokyo, was more impressed by the aerial display of might than his American counterparts. He was on board the *Shawmut* as an observer when the *Ostfriesland* was bombed and sunk.

Ironically, when the Japanese raid on Hawaii's battleship row occurred two decades later, the *Shawmut* – renamed *Oglala* – was sunk at her berth during the attack. Also damaged was the *Pennsylvania*, which was largely protected by being in dry-dock. And also present, but already underway in the harbor and headed for California, was the *Henderson*; she escaped unscathed.

Perhaps July 21, 1921, was the real day of infamy: the day that forecast the one that President Roosevelt proclaimed on December 7, 1941, when Japanese aircraft bombed the Hawaiian Navy base at Pearl Harbor.

Paukenschlag

The United States was now at war, and the government did not have to choose which side to support. After the United States declared war on Japan – and against her Axis compatriots, Nazi Germany and Italy – the Lend-Lease program became superfluous.

Before the United States had time to establish a war of aggression, Nazi Germany brought the war to the American mainland. The German word "paukenschlag" has been translated a number of ways. Literally, it translates as "beat of a kettledrum." Idiomatically, it has been transliterated as "drum roll" or "drumbeat." By any translation or transliteration, the word has come to mean "the initial attack by U-boats against the North American continent."

Winston Churchill, once again Prime Minister of England, had been right to fear U-boats in World War One. Until the American declaration of war, England and her Allies were taking the brunt of the U-boat carnage. Now the Allies were about the share the wealth – and the stealth – of U-boat bloodshed.

The skipper whom Doenitz chose to spearhead the assault against shipping in Canadian and American waters was Kapitanleutnant Reinhard Hardegen.

Hardegen joined the Kriegsmarine as a cadet in 1932, at the age of 19. After rigorous land-based basic training, the first naval vessel that he felt under his boots was a sailing vessel, where he trained before the mast. After many months of hard training, he was transported to the light cruiser *Karlsruhe*, which was soon to embark on a round-the-world cruise. The ironies of this cruise should not be lost upon readers who are familiar with subsequent history.

The *Karlsruhe* semi-circled England, passed through the Mediterranean Sea and the Suez Canal, visited the subcontinent of India as well as the islands of Sumatra and Java and the continent of Australia, and then landed at Hawaii. At the U.S. Navy base at Pearl Harbor, Hardegen finagled his way aboard an American submarine. Later, at New York Harbor, he took time to tour the City and to take the elevator to the top of the Empire State Building. History does not record whether he was disappointed at not seeing any hand-outs about King Kong's famous visit and subsequent demise.

After the *Karlsruhe* returned to Germany, Hardegen enrolled in the German naval academy, where he excelled in coursework that included not only warship operations and weapons management, but also science and engineering. This year-long study program prepared him for U-boat service. Ironically, after successful completion of all these seafaring courses, he received orders to take pilot training in the non-existent naval air arm.

Hardegen duly excelled in this unwanted schooling. Catastrophe struck when an instructor took him into the air for hands-on training, and the plane crashed during take-off. Hardegen barely survived. He spent six months in the hospital. The long recuperation left him weak and disabled with a permanently bad leg. Nonetheless, after his release from medical treatment, he returned to the naval aviation arm, completed his studies, and became a pilot in Hitler's growing air corps.

Yet, after four years of flying, and after Nazi Germany invaded Poland, Hardegen was yanked out of the aviation service and re-assigned to the also growing U-boat fleet. These were times when Hitler was expanding all of Germany's military branches – land, sea, and air - in preparation for his grand plan to take over the world.

After re-orientation, Hardegen was posted as First Watch Officer on the *U-124*, under the command of Kapitanleutnant George-Wilhelm Schulz.

Keeping in mind that no World War Two U-boat skipper was experienced in combat at the onset of hostilities, you might think that Schulz had a checkered career. His first command was the small coastal Type IIB U-boat, *U-10*, of which he took control prior to Germany's invasion of Poland. After the commence of war, he made two short patrols which resulted in no successful attacks. Nonetheless, he was then promoted in rank and given command of a spacious Type IXB U-boat, *U-64*.

The *U-64* was committed to the invasion of Norway. On the eighth day of the patrol, the *U-64* was spotted off the Norwegian coast by a British biplane torpedo bomber, which could also be rigged as a dive bomber. The plane was capable of carrying only a single bomb or torpedo. In the present instance, the *U-64* was struck fairly by a 350-pound bomb which ruptured the U-boat's watertight hull. The plane then machine-gunned the hull as the Germans sought to abandon the sinking ship.

Eight men were killed, but the remainder of the crew of forty-six was pulled out of the sea by members of the German mountain troops, who rowed their landing boats to the beleaguered men in the icy water as they drifted idly in their inflatable life vests.

Despite his lack of success, the loss of his U-boat, and the death of eight of his men, Schulz was given command another modern Type IXB U-boat, *U-124*. Schulz's fourth patrol demonstrated the promise that U-boat command held for this so-far bad luck skipper. He made a concerted attack against convoy HX-65A off the coast of Scotland, and, although the U-boat was damaged by follow-up depth-charge attacks, he was credited with three "kills" for nearly 15,000 gross tons of Allied merchant shipping.

Schulz conducted four more patrols on the *U-124*. The most successful was his seventh (the U-boat's fourth), during which he was credited with sinking eleven vessels for more than 50,000 gross tons. His least successful was the following patrol, with no credited kills. After that, he accepted a staff position and surrendered the U-boat to his second in command, Johann Mohr. His total career credits amounted to nearly 90,000 gross tons. He was number 40 in the list of the most successful U-boat aces of World War Two.

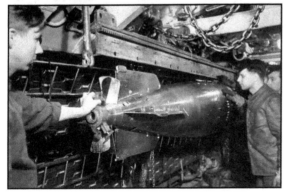

Two German postcard pictures from World War Two.
Above: Maneuvering a torpedo through a torpedo loading hatch.
Below: Performing the nonstop task of torpedo maintenance

Hardegen was on board for Schulz's last two patrols: his best and his worst while in command of the *U-124*. Hardegen was then given his own command: the just-off-the-ways Type IID U-boat, *U-147*. This type U-boat was smaller and more cramped than the American submarines that Hardegen had seen at Pearl Harbor, and must have been somewhat of a disappointment after the disfavor that he expressed after touring an American sub.

Hardegen's initiation as a U-boat skipper was nearly as checkered as that of his predecessor.

In the fading twilight off the coast of Scotland, Hardegen spotted what he thought was an Allied merchant vessel. He wasted no time in launching a torpedo. The torpedo either missed or failed to detonate. The lucky ship was not a merchant vessel but a British destroyer. She turned immediately toward the U-boat and ran down the wake of the torpedo.

Hardegen ordered a crash dive. As the U-boat dipped beneath the surface, the after hatch seal malfunctioned. Hundreds of gallons of seawater rushed into the pressure hull, partially flooding the after compartment and destabilizing the boat. The crew worked desperately to carry water forward in an attempt to regain trim. All efforts failed. With the U-boat plummeting through water that was deeper than the hull's crush depth, Hardegen had to give the order that he dreaded: Surface!

Nazi Germany produced a series of stamps that depicted various wartime scenes. Above is the likeness of a U-boat. Right (on the opposite page) is the likeness of a U-boat commander peering through an attack periscope.

All ballast tanks were blown. The boat's descent slowed, stopped, then commenced to rise. The U-boat surfaced like a broaching whale.

Hardegen opened the control room hatch and climbed into the conning tower. By this time the sky was dark, but the destroyer's silhouette was barely discernible in the nearby water. In these pre-radar days, the destroyer could detect the presence of a U-boat's low hull only by eyesight.

Under the cloak of darkness, the crew effected repairs to the hatch seal while the pumps discharged the accumulated water. The U-boat then submerged and slunk away, to fight again another day.

To add to the U-boat's difficulties, one diesel engine shut down completely while the other barely operated. The mechanics concluded that salt water from the previous flooding had fouled the lubricating oil. While the oil was being changed, Hardegen – ever on the alert – detected a target in the faint light of the rising moon. Because the diesel engines were not operational, Hardegen switched to battery power to drive the electric motors.

Top speed on electric motors was only seven knots. But the target vessel was angling in the direction of the U-boat. Hardegen gave the order to prepare to attack. When the moment was right with respect to distance, speed, and angle, he fired a torpedo. The torpedo struck squarely against the hull. A violent explosion ripped through the nighttime sky, and the unknown vessel quickly slipped beneath the waves.

Hardegen drove the U-boat slowly through the resulting mass of flotsam to which bedraggled survivors clung. He called to them in order to ascertain the name of their vessel, so he could use the sunken tonnage to commence his record of success.

Came the reply, "The Norwegian freighter *Augvald*."

Only in retrospect can modern historians appreciate the irony of this initial "kill" or "success" as being Norwegian. Coincidentally, a U-boat sank another *Augvald* in World War One.

Hardegen then turned the U-boat away from the survivors, and left them to their fate nearly a hundred miles from shore. Of the complement of thirty officers and crewmembers, only one able seaman ultimately survived the ordeal. Rasmus Kolsto was rescued by the HMS *Pimpernel* after he spent eleven days of solitude in a life raft. The fate and suffering of the other Norwegians are unknown. Hardegen traded their lives for the 4,811 gross tonnage that was added to his score card.

After this patrol, Hardegen relieved Kapitanleutnant Karl-Heinz Moehle as skipper of the *U-123*: the U-boat that would bring him fame and with which he will forever be associated in the annals of U-boat warfare.

His first patrol in the spacious Type IXB took him to the west coast

of Africa, where Hardegen committed the worst crime that a U-boat skipper could possibly commit: he sank a neutral vessel.

The Portuguese freighter *Ganda* was proceeding in broad daylight past the coast of Morocco when Hardegen identified her as a British vessel. He fired a torpedo that appeared to have passed astern of the target. By the time the U-boat caught up with the vessel, night had fallen. The next torpedo was aimed with greater accuracy, and struck the hull alongside the engine room. The hull listed to port but did not sink, and the crew stayed tenaciously onboard in an attempt to stop the flooding.

Hardegen grew anxious after a while as the vessel refused to give up the ghost. He therefore pumped another torpedo into the listing hull.

Still the vessel refused to sink. Hardegen gave the order to surface. He then called out the gun crew, and had them fire on the ship. A few well-placed gun shells achieved his goal. The hull rolled over and, in a froth of bubbles, slowly headed for the seabed.

Hardegen did not ascertain the vessel's name. He estimated the tonnage and continued the patrol. Not until he returned to U-boat headquarters, where Doenitz read his deck log and action report, was he apprised of his gross error in judgment.

Meanwhile, over the next couple of months, Hardegen was credited with sinking four or five additional vessels. (Either the facts or the records are unclear.)

Hardegen's next patrol sent him to the North Atlantic. He managed to get a torpedo into the 13,984-gross-ton ocean liner *Aurania*. Escorts forced him to submerge and stay down until the convoy passed. Hardegen surfaced to a sea that was empty except for a capsized lifeboat to which a single survivor clung. Hardegen rescued the survivor, Bertie Shaw. Shaw informed Hardegen that the *Aurania* had sunk. Hardegen was ecstatic about adding so much tonnage to his record.

However, the truth was stranger than fiction. The *Aurania's* captain had ordered the lifeboats swung out on their davits, in preparation for abandoning ship. Shaw and five others had launched the boat accidently, before the order was given to abandon ship. The lifeboat capsized because the liner had too much way on her hull. The British destroyer *Croome* rescued three men, and two others drowned, leaving Shaw alone on the wide, wide sea. After the *Aurania's* crew managed to stay the flooding, the liner proceeded under escort at reduced speed. Shaw purposely lied to Hardegen so he would not chase after the convoy.

This was one way in which facts got twisted in the records. German records showed that the *Aurania* was sunk, while British records showed that the *Aurania* was damaged, repaired, and returned to service.

The *Aurania* was Hardegen's only tonnage claim for the patrol.

Yet even after such a lackluster performance, and after causing an international furor by sinking a neutral vessel, Doenitz handed him the opportunity of a lifetime: to lead what ultimately became the deadliest U-boat or submarine operation in the history of the world.

Doenitz called it Paukenschlag.

First Blood

Now at the age of 28, Hardegen's position as the vanguard of Paukenschlag would enable him to place 24th in the hierarchy of Nazi Germany's highest ranking U-boats aces.

The German roster of vessels and tonnages sunk must be taken with a grain of salt. As we have already seen, Hardegen was credited with the *Aurania's* tonnage of 13,984 gross tons when in actuality he merely damaged the British ocean liner. On the other hand, Germany did not credit him with sinking the neutral Portuguese freighter *Ganda* so as to avoid an international scandal. Nor was he given credit for sinking the Norwegian freighter *Octavian*, even though he actually did sink that vessel; the *Octavian's* tonnage was given to Kapitanleutnant Rolf Mutzelburg of the *U-203*.

I do not intend these observations to be a critique. I wish only to emphasize the confusion that occurred when U-boat attacks and tonnage credits were assigned without absolute positive proof that a credited vessel was actually sunk, and by whom, and that in some cases a vessel did not sink, or it sank and was later salvaged. I suppose it's possible that in the big picture, these circumstances happened to every U-boat skipper, so that perhaps the tonnage credits and mis-credits averaged out at the end of the war.

Once the United States entered the war against the Axis powers, it gave free rein to Nazi Germany to attack not only American warships and merchant vessels, but all shipping along the American eastern seaboard and the Gulf of Mexico. After all, the amount of oil, food, and supplies that was being shipped from the United States was finding its way either to the front lines of battle, or to England in support of the front lines of battle.

Doenitz's plan was to sink Allied ships at their source instead of waiting for them to cross the Atlantic Ocean, where they were better protected by the British navy.

Because France had fallen to the Nazi blitzkrieg in June of 1940, French ports were available for use as U-boat docks. The *U-123* departed from Lorient on December 23, 1941. According to Hardegen's log, "Steered a course on the great circle for *Nantucket* lightship." Hardegen and his men celebrated Christmas in the Bay of Biscay: that huge body of quiescent water that was bordered on the east by France and on the south by Spain. Deck log:

> Trees were placed in all compartments, decorated by the crew and provided with electrical candles. Later the real trees were in some cases replaced by artificial trees. After a collective ceremony and subsequent meal, the letters, packets and goody bags were distributed. It was celebrated in the individual compartments and one could hear the old Christmas songs performed by the crew. The war was forgotten for a few hours by this simple but impressive Christmas festival.

Hardegen's instructions called for him to keep his presence a secret until he arrived off the eastern seaboard. After slipping through the British blockade, the *U-123* faced a three-thousand-mile passage across the Atlantic Ocean.

It is interesting to note that a photojournalist accompanied the *U-123* on this historic mission, much like the scenario that was posited in the German movie *Das Boot* (1981).

Hardegen deviated slightly from his course after the radio operator intercepted an SOS from the *Dimitrios Inglessis*, whose rudder had fallen off. By the time the *U-123* arrived on the scene, the salvage tug *Foundation Franklin* already had the tug under tow and was proceeding to Halifax under the escort of two Canadian destroyers. Hardegen attempted to get into position to take out one of the destroyers before going for the freighter that would have added 5,275 tons to his score card, but due to moonlight and intermittent fog, he wisely did not engage the enemy.

Otherwise, the transatlantic crossing was uneventful until just before he reached his assigned area of operations.

In the post-midnight darkness of January 12, 1942, some two hundred miles south-southeast of Cape Sable, Hardegen spotted a target that he could not ignore: the British ocean liner *Cyclops*. The aged liner had been built in 1906. She weighed in at 9,076 gross registered tons: a fat target for any U-boat skipper to bag if he wanted to increase his tonnage reputation, even if he had to ignore his orders to do so. Despite her slow speed of 13 knots, she had survived two U-boat attacks during the Great War. Now she was a sitting duck for a U-boat that could almost match her speed.

Hardegen fired a torpedo that struck the hull slightly abaft the smokestack. The ship took a gradual list to port, and settled somewhat by the stern. Passengers and crew started to abandon ship. Yet after a while, the hull seemed to have reached a state of balance. Lifeboats commenced to return to the damaged liner.

The U-boat's radio operator intercepted the *Cyclops'* call for help. This probably meant that Canadian patrol vessels were already on the way and could appear at any time. Nonetheless, afraid that the damaged liner might be towed to safety, Hardegen navigated the *U-123* into position for the coup de grace. The second torpedo struck the hull forward of the wheelhouse. The *Cyclops* sank five minutes later, forcing stragglers who had not had time to launch lifeboats or rafts to leap for

This emergency life raft is supporting a survivor of the *Cyclops*. The man is unconscious but alive. (From *Life* magazine.)

their lives into the icy water.

Twenty hours after the *Cyclops* sank, the Canadian minesweeper *Red Deer* plucked freezing and frostbitten survivors from rafts and lifeboats. Of 191 passengers and crew, 94 men, women, and children perished in the ordeal.

Such was the opening shot of Paukenschlag: the devastating portent of the hundreds of lost vessels and thousands of human fatalities that were to follow in Hitler's mad scheme to enslave the planet, and to kill all those who interfered with the achievement of his goal.

Eastern Sea Frontier

The ESF was a U.S. Navy wartime operational designation that included the Atlantic Ocean offshore of the States from Maine to Georgia inclusive, to approximately 200 miles from the coast. The actual boundaries were somewhat fluid, and changed slightly throughout the war in order to effectively succor vessels in distress and to effect the rescue of survivors of stricken vessels.

Hardegen reached the ESF on January 14, 1942, and entered the realm of American history. The first vessel that he encountered in American-defended waters was the modern 489-foot-long Norwegian tanker *Norness.*

The *Norness* was a steel ship that was full of ironies. Built in 1939 by the Deutsche Werft A.G., of Hamburg, Germany, for the Tanker Corporation, a Norwegian company, she was registered Panamanian: that because after Germany invaded Norway, the company moved its offices to New York and continued to operate on the side of the Allies. The *Norness* was en route from New York City to Halifax, Nova Scotia with a load of fuel oil when, sixty miles off Montauk, Lond Island, New York, a torpedo struck without warning against her port side.

Hardegen had fired two torpedoes but one missed the target.

Captain Hansen was asleep at the time of the attack, but awoke immediately. He pulled an overcoat over his pajamas. "Nobody was expecting a submarine so close in American waters. I think we are just as safe there as in New York Harbor." Hansen revised his opinion at 0137. He rushed onto deck and directed the lowering of all lifeboats, motorboats, and rafts. The decks and tackle were slippery with splattered fuel oil.

The radio operator transmitted an SSS (code letters meaning "attacked by submarine"), but the message was not intercepted. There was no time to man the 4-inch deck gun that was mounted on the after deck platform.

The youngest member of the crew, 17-year-old Egge Bremseth, was blown off the deck when a second torpedo slammed into the starboard side. Kane Reinertsen fell into the frigid sea when a lifeboat capsized during the launching operation. These two men claimed the dubious honor of becoming the first victims of the U-boat war in the ESF.

Sverre Sandandnes was at the helm when the first torpedo exploded. As the ship settled, he scrambled into a lifeboat and was dumped into the freezing water along with Reinertsen. Waves slammed him against the steel hull, but he managed to hold onto the rope falls until he was dragged up on deck. "Was damn cold!"

The tanker was sinking so quickly that when Anton Slettebarg awoke, he had only enough time to grab a life vest, slippers, and a prized gold watch before making good his escape.

Paul Georgsen was sleeping in the mess room when the first torpedo struck. He scrambled in the darkness to search for his pet puppy, a white-haired mongrel named Pete, and the dog's playmate, a kitten. He could not find either of them. When he missed the first lifeboat and fell into the water, he climbed back on deck by himself and returned to the mess room. He found the dog, then ran outside and jumped onto a life raft. Waves washed freezing water in continuous streams over the low gunwales, drenching all on board. The puppy whimpered unmercifully, and shivered so hard that Georgsen knew that it could not survive. "So I said 'good-bye' to him, then brained him on the deck."

Along with five others, Einar Anderson, the second officer, got away on a raft after another torpedo struck. "Then we saw the submarine. It

Thanks go to Ben Roberts for creating this composite of the *Norness* on the surface and underwater. Ben is both a technical diver and side-scan sonar expert. As a result, he has dived on the *Norness* on numerous occasions, and he made the side-scan sonar image of the tanker's stern. The topside photograph is an official U.S. Coast Guard photo. The side-scan sonar image of the bow was made by the National Oceanic and Atmospheric Association. Ben arranged the sonar images so their placement corresponds with the topside photo.

was about seventy-five yards away when it fired five or six shots at us — one for each man on the raft, I guess. We all lay as flat as we could. You know, being on a raft is like being in the water. We swallowed plenty, and we got plenty wet."

Chief Engineer Henry Danielson was not caught unawares. "I was sleeping on a sofa in my pants, shirt and socks. I do not like to go to bed in pajamas on sea in wartime! I jump up and got away in big life boat with twenty-four men. Most of them were half-dressed. Wind was blowing, and was cold like hell!"

The circling U-boat fired a forth torpedo which Hardegen surmised had passed under the hull. He then fired a fifth torpedo – the coup de grace – into the abandoned ship before leaving the area. The *Norness* sank by the stern. As the after end came to rest on the sandy bottom, the hull snapped in two forward of the diesel engine room. The forward section, buoyed by its watertight cargo tanks, "became a grounded derelict." Forty feet of the bow protruded out of the water at an awkward angle.

Captain Hansen rallied his men to remain in the vicinity of the wreckage. This was impossible for the raft, as it had no sails or means of propulsion, so it slowly drifted away with the current. Cold and wet, thirty-eight officers and men suffered the abuse of the open sea, awaiting rescue. The men were inadequately protected from the elements, exposed as they were to the wind and to the spray of a developing sea. Those in the raft suffered incalculably more; they were constantly drenched by waves that washed cruelly over the low sides.

For the rest of the night and all the next morning, the motor launch and lifeboat remained by the partially sunken tanker. Gobs of oil rose to the surface from the ruptured tanks, creating a slick on the surface of the sea.

Not until that afternoon did a patrol plane spot the itinerant raft twenty-five miles north of the still-floating bow. The call for help brought another plane that "located raft adrift with six persons on board. Dropped food and restoratives."

Soon thereafter, Navy blimp *K-6* arrived and performed sentinel duty by hovering over the raft as an aerial marker until the arrival of rescue vessels: the Coast Guard cutter *Argo*, which was dispatched from the naval base at Newport, Rhode Island, and the destroyer *Ellyson*, which was rerouted from her patrol area. The *Ellyson* rode shotgun as the *Argo* picked up the life raft that was occupied by the six crewmembers.

Meanwhile, the fishing smack *Malvina D.* rescued Captain Hansen and the rest of the officers and crew. By the time the *Argo* and *Ellyson* reached the wreck site, the *Malvina D.* was on her way to her homeport at New Bedford, Massachusetts.

After a thorough search of the area, the *Argo* returned to Newport, where she disembarked the survivors. The merchant seamen were hospitalized for exposure.

The survivors of the *Norness* found kindness awaiting them in their allies. Because the men had lost everything they owned, the American Friends of Norway donated gifts including knitted woolen socks, sweaters, scarves, and overcoats. Georgsen, who had lost his little dog and kitten, was given a month-old spitz puppy. Ironically, the spitz was a breed that originated in Germany.

Meanwhile, Hardegen did not let any barnacles grow on his hull. The *U-123* lurked nearby, listening to radio chatter. He got in position to let loose another torpedo at a large freighter, but was able to identify her as the Spanish vessel *Isla De Tenerife* before firing, so he let her continue unmolested. At that time Spain was officially neutral but supported the Axis powers.

The *U-123* headed toward the New York-New Jersey bight. Due to faulty and seemingly intentional reporting after the war, urban legend has it that Hardegen drove his U-boat into New York harbor, and went so far as to disembark and walk around New York City to see the sights. What balderdash! But many people believe this grossly fictitious story and continue to spread the absurdity, perhaps because they would like it to be true. Hardegen's deck log contradicts the tale:

> Ahead land in sight. Many lights visible. Seems to be a suburb of New York, whose bright glow is clearly seen on the horizon. Distance from the center of the city about 30 miles. The *Ambrose* lightship is also not on station. I have 11 meters of water under the keel. It must not get much shallower, because I would not be able to get the conning tower under water.

Straight from the horse's mouth. Hardegen and I rest our case! In the dark hours of the morning of January 15, before the Ameri-

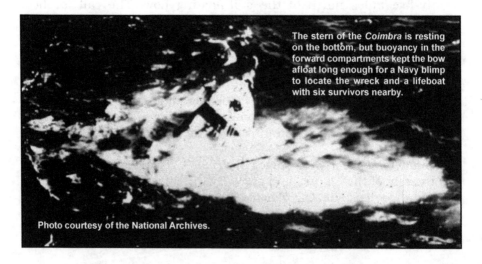

The stern of the *Coimbra* is resting on the bottom, but buoyancy in the forward compartments kept the bow afloat long enough for a Navy blimp to locate the wreck and a lifeboat with six survivors nearby.

Photo courtesy of the National Archives.

Above is an official U.S. Coast Guard photo. Ben Roberts took the side-scan sonar image of the wreck, and created the composite in which the layout of the wreck corresponds to the topside picture.

can public had the opportunity to read about his exploits with the *Norness*, Hardegen torpedoed the British tanker *Coimbra*. Deck log:

> The effect was stunning. A fierce detonation, a column of fire rose over 200 meters high and the whole sky was as bright as day. For many seconds the sea and horizon around us was clearly visible. Compared to this the *Norness* was just mediocre fireworks. The bridge was burning and it was therefore not possible to use the radio. He seems bigger than the *Norness*, especially the superstructure on the stern. Amazingly long. He is surely 10,000 tons GRT. Now quickly a coup de grace to prevent being disturbed, because this fiery glow has to be seen from New York. [It was not.]
>
> Forewarned by the experiences yesterday he got a clean coup de grace from the tube V in the stern underneath the funnel. Hit after 45 seconds. This was good because he had a gun aft where flashlights could be seen. We were clearly visible to him due to the fire aboard. Heavy detonation, high columns of fire, black mushroom cloud. Settles fast by the stern and sinks.
>
> Stern hits the bottom at 54 meters. This time, the bow protrudes from the first mast at an angle of about 30° out of the water. These are some pretty buoys we are leaving for the Yankees in the harbor approaches as replacements for the lightships.

Hardegen's glowing and glowering description of the raging conflagration neglected to mention any feelings for the men who were burned to death in the flames.

Details of the experiences of the crewmembers were meager as most of them were incinerated when the cargo of lubricating oil caught fire and the tanker became a charnel house. Despite flames raging throughout the ship, half a dozen men managed to launch a lifeboat and make good their escape. Thirty-six men perished in torment.

Again, first word arrived over the airwaves when a patrol plane spotted the *Coimbra's* survivors in a dory, south of Shinnecock Inlet, Long Island. High winds, whipping seas, and bitter cold hampered an intensive search-and-rescue effort. As with the *Norness* incident, a Navy blimp located the wreck floating bow out of the water. The blimp dropped restoratives and other supplies to the sorely exposed seamen, and hovered as a marker until the U.S. destroyers *Mayrant* and *Grayson* arrived on the scene to rescue the six freezing survivors.

Hardegen's estimate of the tanker's tonnage was like that of a fisherman telling his friends about the size of his catch. The *Coimbra* grossed 6,768 tons. Perhaps he was deceived by the mass of flames that distorted the silhouette.

By now, newspapers spread the word across the country that the United States was under attack. Both naval and aerial patrols were increased. The next day, the *U-123* was caught on the surface during daylight. Deck log:

> Crash-dive for aircraft that came out of the haze on port side. 4 aircraft bombs to starboard. They were badly aimed. The Yankees have much to learn.

Hardegen found no targets of opportunity as he meandered southward along the New Jersey coast and entered the waters off Delaware. But this did not mean that there was no action afloat. Dense nighttime fog accounted for the collision between the *San Jose* and the *Santa Elisa* (described in Chapter 3). The bow of the *Santa Elisa* cut hard into the hull of the *San Jose* with such force that the rending hull plates created sparks that ignited the cargo in the former's forward hold. The *Santa Elisa* transmitted an SOS, and shot flares into the sky. Both the flames and the flares were visible from shore. Thus the first fire at sea that was observed from American beaches was the result of a maritime accident, not enemy action.

Although enemy action was occurring, only the crew of the *U-123* was aware of it. As the U-boat passed the mouth of the Delaware Bay, Hardegen spotted "Star shells on starboard abeam." He must have seen the flares from the *Santa Elisa*. A few hours later he spotted the navigation lights of the *Octavian*, as described in Chapter 3. There is no need to repeat that information here.

Hardegen torpedoed and sank the *Octavian*, but no one in U-boat headquarters believed him. Neither did the Allied Assessors, nor Jurgen

Rohwer. Not until Sean Manni discovered the wreck, and Rusty Cassway identified it, did the world come to accept that Hardegen was right all along.

The Treadmill

Hardegen was no longer the only U-boat that was operating in the Eastern Sea Frontier. Doenitz had been able to scrape together six U-boats for the initial attack, and more were to come. Many more.

Next in line was the *U-66*, then the *U-130*, then the *U-125*, then the *U-106*, then the *U-109*. And after the original half dozen, others were being prepared and dispatched to the happy hunting waters of the Americas.

The *U-66* was the first to pass the *U-123* and reach the rich pinch-point off the Diamond Shoals of North Carolina. It torpedoed and sank the tanker *Allan Jackson* on January 18, and the ocean liner *Lady Hawkins* on January 19.

Yet Hardegen came on with a vengeance on January 19. In a single night of fury he fought against three Allied vessels off the Outer Banks of North Carolina: the passenger-freighter *City of Atlanta*, the tanker *Malay*, and the freighter *Ciltvaira*.

He reached the Outer Banks too close to sunrise to make any attacks. Deck Log:

> What a pity to have 3 big ships in sight at dawn without getting closer. Maneuver to perhaps sink the outbound tanker.
>
> I could not attack. That was bad luck. But the area seems to be rich with targets and if he has not seen me, there will be enough other steamers here tomorrow.

Deck log later:

> According to hydrophone reports there are still many steamers running along. I want to get close to the shore and wait directly off Cape Hatteras. Again a starlit sky and calm seas. It should be possible to use my remaining 5 torpedoes.
>
> A light to starboard. Go for it! Freighter of approximately 4000 GRT. 4 hatches, heavily loaded. Speed 9-10 knots.

There were ships everywhere. In orderly succession, Hardegen attacked the *City of Atlanta* at 0207, the *Malay* at 0230, and the *Ciltvaira* at 0500.

The *City of Atlanta* was a passenger-freighter that was headed south from New York City to Savannah, Georgia with a general cargo. Second Officer George Tavelle was one of only three survivors; his testimony, taken in the hospital, is the keenest insight into the calamity. "There was no moon. It was a starlit night; smooth sea. . . . Our lights were

U.S.S. CITY OF ATLANTA
AUG. 1, 1917.   NEG# 1498

The *City of Atlanta* was launched in 1904 as a passenger/freighter. In addition to staterooms that occupied the two upper decks, with both a shaded and sunlit promenade, her cargo holds were large and commodious, and usually filled with general merchandise. She worked largely in the coastal trade. The text in the lower left corner states that the picture was taken on August 1, 1917: shortly after America's entry into World War One. "U.S.S." stands for "United States Ship," and implies that she was registered in the U.S. Navy. There is no mention of the *City of Atlanta* in the multi-volume *Dictionary of American Naval Fighting Ships*: only one of thousands of oversights and errors in both the printed and online versions. I found multiple mentions in other sources that cite crewmembers who served on her during the war, including gunners who manned the deck gun on the bow. That gun was emplaced only during World War One. She was unarmed at the time she was torpedoed by the *U-123*. (Courtesy of the National Archives.)

dimmed on Navy Department instructions." He was on watch when "the ship was struck on the port side, a little abaft of the engine room bulkhead in No. 3 hold. There was a great flare of flame on the explosion, and there was debris in the air, and a very heavy concussion. The concussion blew in the pilot house windows, shattering them. Fragments of glass struck me on the forehead, inflicting a cut over the right eye. I didn't get a chance to see what other damage was done aft of the pilot house, but Mr. Fennell has told me that the explosion blew in the house along the port side. A piece of the wreckage on which I floated until picked up was the frame of the port dining salon door."

The *City of Atlanta* took an immediate port list. A minute later, Tavelle had to kick his way through the jammed pilothouse door. "The men were already gathering on the deck when I came out on the starboard side, and with considerable difficulty, because of the rapid listing of the ship to port, we managed to get Nos. 1 and 3 boats swung out, but by the time the davits were swung out the ship had listed to port so sharply that the boats rested on the starboard side and we could not release the grips. . . . Within ten minutes – not more – after the explosion the ship turned over. She first lay on her port side for a moment or two and then turned keel up.

"While I was on the starboard side getting boats out, and I should say between four and five minutes after the impact, the submarine came around our stern and up on our starboard quarter and stood off perhaps seventy-five feet from where we were in the boats, but close under the stern. She played a small searchlight over us and it was still on us when the ship was turning over and I got into the water. . . . For some time after the ship had turned over and we were in the water, the submarine remained in the near vicinity completely surfaced. She then showed running lights and a foremast light which she had not shown when I saw her immediately after the impact and when we were still aboard the ship. Though there were a number of men around the submarine in close proximity calling for help, I saw nothing to indicate that any effort was put out to save any of the crew.

"Just before the ship turned on its side I was standing on the rail trying to release the jammed falls. One of them slipped and broke my hold, and I fell into the water on the starboard side in the space between the two life boats. I managed to get out from between the boats and swam away from the ship, and presently I picked up a piece of wreckage on which I floated until I was picked up. I was picked up by the *Seatrain Texas* shortly before nine o'clock Monday morning, January 19th. I figure that I was in the water between six and seven hours."

Robert Fennell, an oiler, was asleep when the torpedo struck and burst open his locker, spewing out his clothing and personal belongings. He hastily donned a pair of trousers and a sheepskin coat, then clambered on deck to his lifeboat station on the port side. As the ship rolled over, waves washed over the steeply canted deck. With the lifeboat stuck, he jumped free, but the belt of his coat caught in something

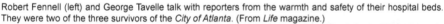

Robert Fennell (left) and George Tavelle talk with reporters from the warmth and safety of their hospital beds. They were two of the three survivors of the *City of Atlanta*. (From *Life* magazine.)

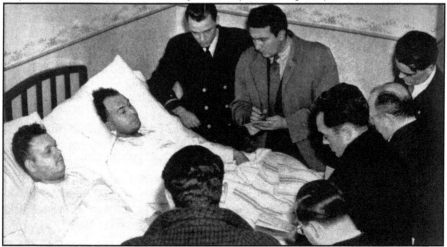

and he was dragged under water as the freighter sank. Fennell held his breath and struggled, finally breaking free and bobbing to the surface. He reported that the ship went down without any suction. He held onto a skylight at first, then transferred to a bench from the crew's dining room.

Also rescued by the passing steamer was Able Bodied Seaman Earl Dowdy. Forty-four men lost their lives, either in the initial explosion or by drowning. Tavelle recalled seeing at least eighteen men clinging to wreckage, slowly weakening, slipping off one by one into the sea, to lie face down as if embracing death.

Later, when examining Tavelle in the hospital, doctors found numerous glass cuts from the shattered bridge windows, as well as a deep gash on his leg, which he got during his fall from the sinking hull. But they were unable to explain his badly discolored neck. Said Tavelle, "I got that from turning around in the water so often trying to see a ship."

Hardegen wasted no time on the *City of Atlanta*. Having observed the ship going under, he left the survivors to their fates and pressed a surface attack on the tanker *Malay*.

Chambliss Holston, able bodied seaman, said, "The first sign of the attack was a crash of glass, and I thought that one of the skylights on deck had fallen and been shattered." The shell struck the bridge, inflicting injuries on those inside, and damaging a lifeboat and setting it on fire. The second shell carried away the port bridge wing.

Captain John Dodge ordered evasive action and full speed ahead. The *Malay* veered away from the U-boat. The short engagement left one man with a broken back, one with a broken collarbone, and several others with broken arms, legs, and fingers. A few minor fires were quickly doused. The *Malay* made off in the darkness. All other ships in the area heeded her radio warning by switching off their lights.

Hardegen pursued the stricken tanker. Forty-five minutes later, three more shells struck the *Malay* aft. In addition to setting the stern partly ablaze, one shell crashed through a bulkhead over the bunk of Adams Hay, a cook. He was killed instantly by the blast. Only because the *Malay* was traveling without cargo was the ship saved from being engulfed in flames like the other tankers.

Three men scrambled into a lifeboat, taking the man with the broken back. The forward lines fouled, the lifeboat capsized, and all were drowned.

Hardegen was persistent and launched a torpedo that struck amidships, flooding No. 7 tank. The *Malay* slowed but maintained her course. Captain Dodge fired flares so that Coast Guard cutters, alerted by radio and already on their way, could locate his ship. Hardegen broke off the attack. The Coast Guard removed three seriously injured men, plus Hay's body, and raced to Norfolk. The *Malay* limped along behind, under escort, and eventually reached Newport News, Virginia under her own power. She went to sea again after $170,000 in repairs.

At 0500, Hardegen torpedoed the Latvian freighter *Ciltvaira*, traveling southbound fully lighted from New York City to Savannah, Georgia. Coal passer Friederich Lusis came out on deck for a breath of air that saved his life. At his station below, two firemen, Rolf Semelin and Carl Gustaefssen, were killed instantly by the blast.

Nick Creteu related his story: "All of a sudden something happened. The whole night was filled with fire. Some kind of a noise happened. I don't know how to say it. I was knocked straight up off my feet, about two feet in the air. But it didn't knock me out."

Rudolf Musts, the radio operator, was locked in his room by torqued bulkheads. "The door was jammed. Everything was black out and ev-

Damage to the *Malay*. Below left: Captain John Dodge stands in the remains of the wheelhouse. Below right: Seaman Nick Athens points to a shell hole in a hull plate. Bottom: The force of the torpedo's explosion tore rivets out of their holes and shoved hull plates upward. (From *Life* magazine.)

The *Ciltvaira* under tow of the *Sciota* while the *Osprey* maintains a position astern of the freighter. (Courtesy of the National Archives.)

erywhere was hot steam. I managed, somehow, to force open the door and that way I got to a lifeboat."

Able Bodied Seaman Leon Lusis (no relation to Friederich) was awakened by the tremendous explosion: "I ran on deck, tried to get in a port lifeboat, but found that our ship had been hit right amidships and that the lifeboat was no good. The crew entered a large starboard lifeboat, which was launched before the captain and the officers of the ship followed in a smaller boat. Before leaving they got the log and the ship's manifest."

Of the thirty-two-man crew, thirty got away. Among the survivors were the ship's mascots: a cat named Briska and a dog named Pluskis. The two lifeboats floated nearby the still-floating *Ciltvaira* for three hours.

The northbound passenger liner *Coamo* passed close aboard the lifeboats and the nearby *Ciltvaira*. The survivors signaled for help by waving flashlights. The *Coamo's* master was evidently aware of the new dangers off the coast. He passed the beleaguered men at full speed. Captain Nels Helgesen was wise to be cautious. Before the end of the year his ship was sunk with all hands – 134 souls – by the *U-604*.

An hour later, the *Ciltvaira* and her lifeboats were spotted by the Standard Oil tanker *Socony Vacuum*, which rescued her fellow mariners.

Captain Skarlis Kerbergs saw that his ship was not settling any farther, so he rallied a boatload of volunteers to return to the vessel.

The only crewmember who spoke fluent English (among a crew of Finns, Danes, Estonians, Dutch, Swedes, Latvians, and a Rumanian) was twenty-year-old Leon Da Salva, a mess boy from British Guiana. In an interview, he said, "After we left the ship, we saw she wasn't going down right away. So one of the boats went back at about seven o'clock to see the damage. We also took out the passports and the ship's papers. We hoisted a signal flag – SOS – and went back to the boat again. We looked back and saw now the ship was broken in the middle with a big hole. She was filling fast with water."

Captain Julio Soares, master of the *Bury*, heard the radio broadcast from fifteen miles away. "The *Ciltvaira* was still floating when I found her. . . . I sent four of my crew to the *Ciltvaira*, in charge of that ship's first officer, in order to pass the cables. It was not until 7 P.M. when all was set for us to tow. Then we started slowly toward Norfolk [Virginia]. We were using three manila and one steel cable. The cables broke at 9 P.M. because of the rough seas.

"There were no lights whatever on the unfortunate vessel because all of her machinery was out of order, so we waited until 11 P.M. Then a heavy fog descended. There was nothing to do but leave her and advise other ships and radio stations of the position of the derelict."

Added Leon Lusis: "The ship was then practically sinking under us. We had to take out our boat again and we were picked up by the Brazilian freighter *Bury*."

Almost completely submerged, the *Ciltvaira* continued to drift. Next to arrive on the scene was the USS *Osprey*. She stood by the settling freighter while the ocean-going tug USS *Sciota* resumed the tow. According to reports, the *Ciltvaira* did not settle completely to the bottom until the twenty-first of the month.

The Clavaria back is broken. (Courtesy of the National Archives.)

It is interesting to contrast the victim's accounts above with the victor's deck log below:

According to hydrophone reports there are still many steamers running along. I want to get close to the shore and wait directly off Cape Hatteras. Again a starlit sky and calm seas. It should be possible to use my remaining 5 torpedoes there. A light to starboard. Go for it! Freighter of approximately 4000 GRT. 4 hatches, heavily loaded. Speed 9-10 knots. Overtaken and due to the bright night and controlled his course of 0°. Overtaken on his starboard side at maximum speed. We are now close to a light buoy north-west of the Wimble Shoal buoy. 3 steamers come towards us. I hope to catch them afterwards. I now get so close that, even if he spots me, he can't avoid me anymore.

Fired from a distance of 450 meters. Target angle 90°, enemy speed 9 knots. After 30 seconds hit aft of funnel. Heavy detonation. Steamer settles aft fast. Stern hits bottom, the bow is visible at a steep angle from the first mast. Chased the others at maximum speed.

Light to starboard. I let the others go and operate on this new target because I am ahead of it.

The light proves to be a small coastal steamer, so I let him go. The channel is marked by light buoys, which the steamers keep on their port side so I decided to follow the buoys and soon see a light starboard ahead. Turned towards it. A steamer of about 4000 GRT. 4 hatches. Speed measured at 10 knots. The situation was clear. I had his course because he was navigating along the buoys. At the Wimble Shoal buoy he turns to 180° so I fall back. Soon I am ahead again and turn towards him to catch up before the Cape [Hatteras] because there he will be able to turn away to starboard again. Water depth 7-8 meters. I want to obtain guaranteed hits with the last 3 torpedoes so I move closer.

Fired torpedo at a distance of 250 meters. Target angle 90°. Due to the shallow water I set depth at 2 meters to prevent the torpedo from hitting the bottom. Torpedo jumps twice out of the water, becomes a surface runner and hits aft. Good that I was that close otherwise the surface runner would have missed astern. Very heavy detonation after 15 seconds. On the bridge one could hear the whistling of debris flying past and falling all around the boat into the water. Steamer settles fast by the stern, heavy list to port. While I do a victory lap, the steamer capsizes to port with the funnel and masts hitting the water. He lies on the bottom with the stern under water and the bow protruding out of the water. Behind me are several lights, so I head north to get the steamers between me and the well lit coast which can be clearly seen. I see 5 vessels in a long line with their lights on. The foremost I recognize as . . . [text illegible] . . . no torpedo but I still have a deck gun. On battle stations for artillery attack, deck gun ready! I position myself directly in his wake. The other 4 steamers sufficiently away (distance 2000 meters). I want to get closer from astern and ambush him when passing.

Open fire! Everything works fantastically, at least 6 hits after in the engine room. Tanker stops and burns. Now I recognize that he is even bigger, about 4000 GRT. He has a slight list to port and because he is on fire I believe he has enough for now and decide to attack the other steamers with torpedoes. Try to overtake a freighter, 6000 GRT, but his speed is 14-15 knots and I barely get ahead. Another one approaches me head-on on a course to the north. I am changing target and try to get closer, but this one is also too fast and because the day is dawning soon I will not be able to fire on him before dawn. But I have others to choose from. My tanker reports by radio message that he is still burning after being attacked by a U-boat with artillery and the "I. Naval Station" should be notified. It was the *Malay* (8207 GRT). I never would have guessed that he is so big. Well, then my last torpedo should be his coup de grace. First another shot on a freighter of 5000 GRT, which is running towards me at 9 knots and I am ahead. One diesel engine broke down due to a rupture of the cooling water piping, so I continue with the other engine on maximum speed.

Fired torpedo. Distance 450 meters, target angle 90°, enemy speed 9 knots. Hit aft of funnel and he breaks in two. He has had enough. Water depth 10 meters. He was heavily loaded. With this one the boat as exceeded the 200,000 tons barrier and I my 100,000 tons. Now fast to *Malay*, which managed to extinguish the fire and reported by radio message that she was operational again. Set off in the approximate direction by instinct. We were lucky. Soon we noticed the smell of a ship burning. Followed the smell and saw two shadows stopped ahead. Go for it! Shortly before we arrive the tanker proceeds on course 340° in the direction of Norfolk. The other steamer *City of Delhi* (7443 GRT) is recovering a lifeboat. I could easily fire on this stopped steamer, but it annoyed me that the tanker was underway again and I wanted to spoil his joy over it. Besides that he was more valuable. While I chased after him, the last torpedoed steamer fires bright white star shells.

I am almost parallel to *Malay*. Something is still burning underneath the deck, but he makes 11 knots. That is stunning. And then he sees me against the bright morning sky. He illuminates me with a spotlight, sends "UD" and turns away hard to port. I turn to starboard. Directly ahead of me is another steamer. In this case he will get the torpedo. Then the *Malay* turns back. Of course, otherwise he would sail right into the coast.

I turn hard to port and fire my last torpedo while turning. After 28 seconds a fierce detonation. Hit just ahead of engine room. Blame yourself for sending a hasty report of about being operational. We are monitoring the 600 meter frequency. But now both engines are at maximum speed. The unusable diesel engine was ready again by welding the ruptured piping. Course 90°. It is already fairly bright, but in 10 meters of water diving is not possible. Still there are many steamers around here. A big tanker is running ahead of me, a giant on the port side. They of course see me, but this does not help. The giant turns towards us and tried to ram. This idea had not occurred to me. I thought he would just run away. Distance 400 meters. Diesel engines on emergency speed. Water depth 20 meters. This is too shallow to crash-dive from maximum speed, he will ram us. It was the Norwegian *Kosmos II* (16,966 GRT). This one we would have enjoyed sinking too. From his radio messages we know that he first believed that we were chasing him, but then he chased us because he thought that there was "something wrong" with us. Without submarine experience he could not know that we are not able to crash-dive in 20 meters of water. Very slowly the distance increases and after 2 hours he gives up because he is in ballast and could not keep up the high speed with empty tanks. We bluff him with a northerly course, which he immediately reports. Furthermore he sends the exact position and bearing signals. At 13.20 hours, aircraft took off. In this visibility we should see them in time. After he turned away and got out of sight I change course to 160°. All the time the *Malay* sent: "SOS sinking rapidly, next ship please hurry, torpedoed, sinking." He sends frantically "hurry, hurry next ship." Two men were killed and two other badly injured. Therefore we can count him as completely destroyed. The night of the long knives was over. A beat of the drum with 8 ships, among them 3 tankers with 53,060 GRT. . . .[text illegible] . . .

. . . and tonight instead of me with 10 to 20 U-boats present. I believe everyone would have had enough targets. I had seen about 20 steamers, some of them with lights and additionally a few colliers. All en route close to the shore. All [navigation] lights were burning, admittedly darkened, so that they were only visible from 2-3 nm [nautical miles]. That's why U-66 got the impression on the 18th that everything is darkened around here. The surveillance of the 600 meter frequency proved itself, since I knew about the withdrawal of the lightships and knew the

identification signals of the buoys. Moreover I had a good overview about the shipping concentration and situation from the
radio messages by taking a bearing on the steamers. However,
after the first sinkings the shipping was reduced sharply. For
example, the whole private telegram communication of sea-fa-
ring Jews stopped completely.

Thus ended Hardegen's account of the final hours of his participa-
tion in the shooting gallery that the Nazi's called Paukenschlag. Both
sides recorded events the way they experienced or remembered them
in the heat of battle.

The job of the Allied Assessors was to reconcile the differences between the two accounts in accordance with information that was
gleaned long after those events occurred. Hardegen believed that the
Malay must have sunk after the terrible punishment that he inflicted
upon her. The *Malay's* tonnage was added to his score card. Yet against
all odds – and despite being shelled, torpedoed, and partially incinerated – the *Malay* limped into safe harbor under her own power, and
lived to fight another day.

Somehow, the clear description of the loss of the *Octavian* was ignored or overlooked. She was placed in a location where she never
would have gone. Her tonnage was given to a U-boat that was nowhere
in the vicinity of her actual loss. Today the records stand corrected.

But correcting the records does not bring those lost Norwegian
sailors back from the dead. It only places their demise in the appropriate graveyard. It matters not to those Norwegian sailors, nor to their
families and heirs, who got credit for killing them. They were still just
as dead.

Homeward Bound

Hardegen's attacks against Allied shipping in the Eastern Sea Frontier paints a dark picture of him and of the crew who supported him. I
would be remiss if I told only the ruthless parts of his story while ig-
noring other facets that paint him in a different light: a balance, if you
will, in the exigencies of combat.

After all his torpedoes were expended, Hardegen headed for home
via Bermuda, which lay some 600 miles east of North Carolina. He
passed south of the island, then turned northeast in the direction of
France. Deck log entry from January 24:

Just now heard the special announcement about the U-boat
successes off America in which our boat was mentioned by
name.

Received radio message announcing the award of the
Knights Cross to the commander of the *U-123*. In a formal ceremony in the control room, a Knights Cross, hand made by the

crew, which has the 16 ships totaling 110,209 GRT on its back, was awarded to me.

Deck log entry from January 25:

40° to starboard a steamer in sight. Our Sunday roast. His course 220°, speed 9 knots. Overtaken, let him have it!

We are ahead, running towards it. It is a small steamer with a frame around the bow for the use of minesweeping equipment. Heavily loaded, with deck cargo in crates. . . . [text illegible] . . . one gun, about 50 mm [millimeters] with protective shield. About 600 meters behind him. Deck gun ready and opened fire. The first shots hit the stern, then one each under the bridge and in the engine room. Steamer mans the gun and fires. The firing pin of our MG C30 [anti-aircraft gun] is broken, so we fired with the deck gun at his gun. Several hits underneath, but he continues to fire until a direct hit struck the pivot. Gun crew out of action, the barrel can't be moved any more.

We received 5 hits, which did not penetrate the pressure hull. Because they hit very low, I assume that they fell short, burst on the surface and only the splinters hit our hull. some shots passed between conning tower and deck gun, one could hear them whistling past.

Ship is releasing steam, bridge is burning and the crew is abandoning ship in the lifeboats. Strangely they did not release the two big rafts that are intact on great slipways over the foremost and rearmost hatches. Perhaps because they were on the side we fired on.

Replaced the firing pin of the 20 mm AA [anti-aircraft] gun. We fire a single shot into the scenery to test the weapon. This shot exploded in the barrel, apparently due to a defect in the manufacture of the round. Premature detonation Special leader Art.Mt. Toelle is unfortunately hit by shrapnel on the back of his head and fell to the deck bleeding badly. MtrOGfr. Vonderschen has a 5 cm flesh wound on the left thigh, which is harmless. Not the fault of anyone. Vonderschen belonged to the AA gun crew, Toelle was standing near the aft periscope taking photos of the burning steamer. We were firing to right aft. Toelle lost very much blood and had to vomit several times.

The steamer was only able to send "SSS" without name and position. We approach the lifeboats and the first officer told us that the ship was *Culebra* (3044 GRT) from Liverpool loaded with "general cargo." There is water in the boats and the survivors only have one bucket with shrapnel holes in it. We provide them with several buckets and provisions for a few days consisting of bread, lard and sausages and additionally a knife to open the canned food. They have enough water. Gave them the exact position and the course to the Bermudas. The . . . [text illegible] . . . swimming in the water and will be picked up by the boats. On the *Culebra* the signal munitions on the bridge and the ready ammunition for the gun now detonates. Funny looking fireworks with parachute rockets. Bridge collapses. We are shooting holes into the waterline aft. As the stern settles, the deck cargo shifts and we detect aircraft. Wings with a blue-white-red cockade and yellow ring around it, fuselages and tail assemblies. An inflated tire of a landing gear floats on the water. And the gentlemen call this "general cargo"!! Made a few more holes in the after part. Stern sinks, the bow rises and then our ninth steamer sank.

Deck log entry from January 27:

A shadow to starboard, which is soon recognized as a tanker, course 220°, speed 9-10 knots. I overtake and approach from ahead. In this bright moonlight only impudence wins and the trust that his lookouts are inferior to ours. Otherwise he has to see us for I am running at high speed to get closer fast. We must make a decision because a light is seen on the horizon. Subsequently I see a big gun on the stern. I ordered all guns, 105 mm, 37 mm and 20 mm manned . . . [text illegible] . . . Commence the battle from a distance of 2500 meters as crossing action, turning behind his stern to fire from the side. Already the third salvo is on target. Good and fast.

Several hits in engine room and funnel set the stern on fire. There is a flash on the bridge. We get hits on our bridge, which did not penetrate because they hit at a very acute angle. His shots fell short most of the time. Ordered deck gun to be aimed at the bridge and the IIWO soon found the target. Distance now 1000 meters. When the bridge caught fire I turned away sharply to not show my broadside and waited. Tanker stops and launches lifeboats. Radioed position, it is the tanker *Pan Norway* (9231 GRT) sailing in ballast.

While bringing the empty cartridges back into the boat one accidentally fell from the bridge through the control room and hit the MaschOGfr. Bastl in the face and he suffered a split upper lip and lost several teeth. A case of military accident.

After it became clear that the tanker was abandoned, I closed to 250 meters and shot holes into the waterline with the 105 mm gun. The aft gun on the tanker was a 120 mm gun on a high, strong pivot and a well-built platform. According to the survivors it could not be manned due to our fire hitting the stern. There were two machine guns of about 20 mm with protective shields on the bridge which were manned but the gun crews were hit when our first rounds struck the bridge and the guns had to be abandoned.

The tanker sent Morse code by a signal light but we could not read it. We thought that he was capitulating and waited nearby until all men abandoned ship in the lifeboats. After the 105 mm ran out of ammunition we continued to fire into the hull with the 37 mm. He already settled aft with a heavy list to port.

Tanker sank capsizing by the stern. The forward part of the ship is now slowly rising and moves up and down, 40 meters high. In this position it dances a long time up and down . . . [text illegible] . . . and settles a bit. A funny view, scary illuminated by burning oil floating on the sea.

Tanker sank. The light mentioned above turned out to be a neutral steamer, which waited at a distance of 3 nm. We approached him and to our amazement he ran away. We chased after him at maximum speed and ordered him to stop with the signal light, which he did. It was the Greek *Mount Aetna*, underway under the Swiss flag. Went alongside and ordered him to pick up survivors. She followed us to two lifeboats, which we had met earlier, and picked up the men in them.

Then back to the sinking position. Here we found a man drifting in the water and picked him up. The interrogation proved to be difficult because he was wounded by a splinter, exhausted after several hours in the water and spoke only Norwegian. His statements: They were surprised by the war in an English harbor and forced by England to sail for them. The captain was an Englishman and the crew Norwegian. They had been in Halifax from England and were en route to Aruba. As we told him that neither position or course corresponds to this he said that they were out here due to the U-boat danger. They did not see us. After some hits there was apparently some sort of panic aboard. He made it to a lifeboat. The people beat each other for a place and he fell overboard after a "comrade" had hit him hard in the face, they then left him behind. All front teeth were smashed. He was lucky to be found by us and was deeply grateful.

Now we saw that the Swiss ship already turned away. We stopped him again with the signal light and transferred the man. He had taken aboard 29 men and the Norwegians had told the master that the whole crew was there. We knew that he had 51 crew members aboard. It became clear that the Norwegians feared being torpedoed again by us on the *Mount Aetna* and induced the master to leave. We had seen other survivors between debris and the sinking position. We asked the master to turn around and to rescue them too, which he did. He thanks us warmly for not sinking his ship.

Aftermath

Hardegen and the *U-123* returned to the Americas after the first wave of U-boat marauders were succeeded by a second wave, and a third, each one less successful than the previous one. U-boats worked their way south into the Caribbean Sea Frontier and the Gulf Sea Frontier, where they found heavily-laden tankers departing from the rich oilfields on their way to the fighting front in England and Europe.

Scores of Allied vessels were sunk in the ongoing bloodbath, and well-marked neutral vessels as well, for U-boat command blurred the distinction between a vessel's ownership or port of registration and the cargo it was transporting to Allied ports. Now U-boats sank every vessel in sight under Nazi Germany's protocol to shoot first and don't bother to ask questions, ever.

The so-called "happy time" for U-boats lasted only until July 1942 in the Eastern Sea Frontier, and not much later in the neighboring sea frontiers. The number of U-boats that were lost in action rose dramatically, to the point at which the ratio of the number of Allied vessels sunk compared to the number of U-boat's lost was no longer productive for Nazi Germany. U-boat's met such fierce resistance along the American side of the Atlantic that Doenitz dispatched U-boats to the east coast only sporadically. And even then they seldom returned home to tell their tales of woe. The drumbeat soon tolled for the other side.

Hardegen's second foray – off the Florida coast – was as action-packed as his first one, but less successful in that three of the vessels that he attacked either escaped or were later salvaged: *Liebre* (7,057 GRT, escaped), *Oklahoma* (9,264 GRT, salvaged), and *Esso Baton Rouge* (7,989 GRT, salvaged). Thus his exaggerated claim to have sunk more than 75,000 gross registered tons was in reality reduced considerably. Of course, he had no way of knowing about vessels that were salvaged.

However, where he did excel was in the number of casualties that he inflicted. This number was inflated because one of the vessels that he sank was a Q-ship: a seedy looking tramp freighter that was converted to a heavily armed warship, but in such a way that her armament was cleverly concealed behind disguised trapdoors and false structures with collapsible sides. When an unsuspecting U-boat came in for the kill, the naval ensign was raised, the façade fell away, and the fully loaded guns were rolled out and fired.

Hardegen fell into this trap when he fired a torpedo into the hull of the ex-*Carolyn*, in actuality the USS *Atik*. The crew, some dressed as women, faked an abandon ship routine in order to lure the U-boat closer. When Hardegen approached close in order to finish the freighter with artillery, the merchant vessel disguise was dropped and the crew opened fire with a broadside that was far more powerful than that of the U-boat. One German was killed by shrapnel before the U-boat submerged.

But Hardegen did not leave the battle ground (or ocean). He stalked the Q-ship and attacked after dark by firing another torpedo into the *Atik's* hull. The ship sank with all hands: 141 American sailors.

After this patrol, Hardegen relinquished command the *U-123* and took a position in a U-boat training facility. This was followed by a stint with torpedo research and development. Penultimately, he wound up leading an infantry battalion that was fighting against British troops. Thus he had served the Nazi military in the air, on and under the sea, and on land. Just prior to war's end, he accepted a staff position under Doenitz.

After Nazi Germany's capitulation, Hardegen was arrested by British intelligence because his surname was confused with that of an SS (Schutzstaffel) officer whose given name was Paul. The hard-headed British refused to accept Reinhard's passport as proof of his true identity as a U-boat skipper. He was imprisoned for the year and a half that it took for Reinhard and his wife to assemble the documents that were necessary to convince the British that he was who he said he was, and not the Nazi war criminal.

Hardegen became a successful self-employed businessman in civilian life. He died on June 9, 2018 at the age of 105, just three weeks before Sean Manni discovered the *Octavian.*

Before committing suicide – on April 30, 1945 – Adolf Hitler wrote a will in which he promoted, in Hitler's stead, Karl Doenitz to Chancellor of Germany and Supreme Commander of Germany's armed forces. Thus it was left to Doenitz to negotiate the terms of Nazi Germany's surrender to Allied Command barely one week later.

Two of Doenitz's sons were killed in the war.

At the Nuremburg Trials, Doenitz was convicted of various war-crime charges, chief among them being the waging of unrestricted submarine warfare against neutral vessels. He was sentenced to a term of ten years and twenty days, of which he served every day. Upon release, he retired to the small village of Aumuhle, Germany, which measured slightly more than one square mile in size.

Doenitz died on December 24, 1980, aged 89 years.

·-50-AN-127-244 DEC-43
NEWARK DELAWARE
715 BALLASTON AVE
MR H H WOLF

Doenitz's prestige dropped dramatically in *Time Magazine* after the onslaught of Paukenschlag and follow-up U-boat depredations against continental shipping in the Caribbean Sea and the Gulf of Mexico. This new likeness of the admiral is not nearly as flattering as the magazine's earlier depiction, although this one is more realistic.

C5 - "Auf Gefechts=Stationen!"
U-Boot im Einsatz gegen England und Amerika
Kapitanleutnant Reinhard Hardegen

"On Battle Stations!"
Submarine in Action against England and America
by Lieutenant (senior grade) Reinhard Hardegen

This Nazi propaganda book was published in 1943, when the U-boat's supremacy of the sea stood at its high point: a position that was about to change as the hunters slowly became the hunted. Perhaps that was the reason for the book's publication.

The primary reason for the shift in status can be stated in a single word: sonar (in the United States), or asdic (in Great Britain).

Sonar is the acronym for "sound navigation ranging." Asdic is the acronym for "Anti-Submarine Detection Investigation Committee." Sonar works under water the way radar works in the atmosphere. (Radar is the acronym for "radio detection and ranging.") Sonar enabled Allied surface vessels to locate and track U-boats, so they could drop depth charges or hedgehogs on the enemy. If a U-boat was damaged so severely that it was forced to surface, it could then be spotted by radar.

The Allies developed a secondary technology called "high-frequency direction finding." This device was abbreviated as HF/DF; it was pronounced "huff-duff." HF/DF enabled both Allied vessels and land-based stations to detect U-boat radio transmissions. If two or more stations detected a transmission, the position of the transmitting U-boat could be triangulated. A flotilla of Allied naval vessels called a hunter-killer group then converged on the location, refined its position by means of sonar (if the U-boat were under water) or radar (if the U-boat were on the surface), and destroy it by all means necessary.

Hardegen fortuitously avoided becoming a victim in the tremendous U-boat losses that followed his wartime at sea, by being stationed on land; and by luckily not being bombarded by flights of Allied bomber runs that destroyed much of Nazi Germany.

I was unable to read his book because it was published only in German. However, I was able to glean some of his chronology by recognizing place names and the names of vessels that he met at sea. The book is primarily an autobiography of his military career, both as a pilot and a skipper. In keeping with Doenitz's sanitizing orders, the sinking of the neutral vessel *Ganda* was not mentioned.

The photographic section of the book is almost self-explanatory. Nonetheless, I have taken the trouble to translate the captions, by using two online translation sites. A picture may be worth a thousand words, but a few extra words may add valuable description.

Reinhard Hardegen.
Kapitänleutnant.

Reinhard Hardegen - Lieutenant (senior grade)

GROSSADMIRAL KARL DÖNITZ (S. 3
als Befehlshaber der Unterseeboote

Grand Admiral Karl Doenitz - as Submarine Commander

Wo gehobelt wird, da fallen Späne   (S. 22)

Where wood is chopped, splinters must fall

Auf der U-Schule lernten wir das Tauchen   (S. 30)

We learned to dive at the U school

Auslaufen zur Feindfahrt (S. 37)

Leaving for the enemy trip

Es hatte weiter aufgebrist   (S. 40)

It had continued to bristle

Das leuchtende Fanal eines brennenden Dampfers (S. 45)

The glowing of a burning steamer

Das Feuer breitet sich rasch aus (S. 42)

The fire spreads quickly

Der Koppelmaat kontrolliert in der Zentrale an der Karte den Schiffsort   (S. 45)

The coupling mate controls the ship's location on the map at the headquarters

Der Appetit ist großartig — Mittagessen im Bugraum (S. 5

The appetite is large - lunch in the bow

Die Musik war auf der Mole angetreten . . . . . . und ich meldete dem Flottillenchef   (S.64)
The music had started on the jetty   ... and I reported to the flotilla chief

Flagge und Kommandantenwimpel werden   Als Bootswappen hatten wir einen fliegen-
geheißt   (S. 66)   den Fisch   (S. 73)
The flag and the commander's flag are raised   As a boat crest we had a flying fish

Mein erstes Boot   (S. 68

My first boot

Dicke Eiszapfen hingen an Reeling und Netzabweiser   (S. 68

Thick icicles hung on the railing and net deflector

Leutnant (Ing.) Hamisch †   (S. 61)
Lieutenant (engineer) Hamisch

Ein Hilfseisbrecher nahm uns in Schlepp   (S. 75)
An auxiliary ice breaker towed us

Oberleutnant zur See Wetjen † (S. 73)
Lieutenant (junior grade) Wetjen

Mit Wetjen beim Zähneputzen. Wir sahen wie die Seeräuber aus (S. 80)
With Wetjen when brushing teeth. We looked like the seasickers [sic - seasick persons?]

„Auf Gefechtsstationen!" (S. 89)

"On battle stations!"

Die Überlebenden hatten sich auf Flößen und Holzstücken gesammelt (S. 90)
The survivors had gathered on rags and pieces of wool

Von ihnen erfuhren wir, daß es ein Dampfer von 9000 BRT gewesen war (S. 90)
We learned from them that it had been a steamer of 9,000 GRT

Im norwegischen Hafen   (S. 79)

In the Norwegian port

Mittagspause in Norwegen (links der Verfasser, der Obersteuermann, Oblt. z. See Wetjen   (S. 79)

Lunch break in Norway (on the left the author, the helmsman, Lieutenant (junior grade) Wetjen

Eine Bunkeranlage entsteht im Stützpunkt   (S. 101)

A bunker system is being built at the base

ieberhaft wurde am Ausbau gearbeitet . . . (S. 101)
The expansion was worked feverishly

. . und schon bald waren die Bunker im Rohbau fertig (S. 101)
. . . and soon the bunkers in the shell were finished

Auf der Back türmen sich Berge von Kisten und Dosen . . . (S. 104)

On the back towers there are piles of boxes and cans. . .

. . . die alle im Boot verstaut werden sollen (S. 104)

. . . which should all be stowed in the boat

Auslaufen zur Südfahrt   (S. 108)
Leaving to go south

Ein letztes Winken   (S. 107)
One last wave

Tümmler spielen um den Bug des Bootes (S. 112)
Tumblers play for the bow of the boat

Unerbittlich prallte die Sonne auf die Wache (S. 112)
The sun hit the guard relentlessly

„Geschütz klar!"   (S. 110)

"Protection clear!"

„Mit Sprenggranaten laden und sichern!" – Rechts im Bild werden die Granaten von der Rutsche genommen   (S. 110)

"Load and secure with explosive grenades!" - The grenades are removed from the slide on the right

Bald stand er in hellen Flammen (S. 111)

Soon he was on fire

Unser Hannes
Our Hannes

(S. 105

„Kraxel" unterhält uns mit seiner Quetschkommode (S. 116)

"Kraxel" maintains us with his pinch chest [accordion?]

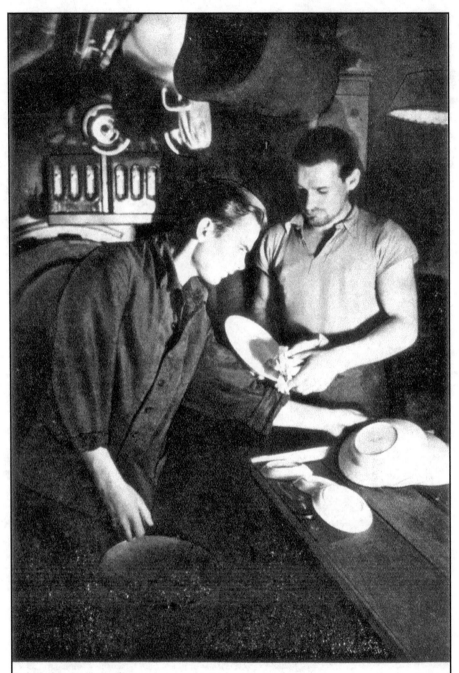

Backschafter im Unteroffizierraum (S. 123)

Pastor in the NCO room [NCO = non-commissioned officer]

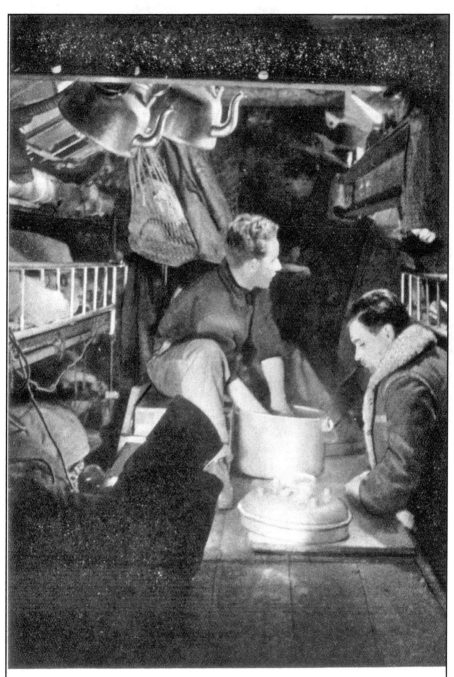

Backschafter im Bugraum (S. 123)

Baker in the bow area

Während wir im Offizierraum „Mensch ärgere dich nicht" spielten . . .
While we were playing in the officer's room "man don't argue" . . .

. . . wurde im U-Raum ein Skat gekloppt   (S. 124)
. . . a skat was knocked in the U-space

Schweinsfische, unsere ständigen Begleiter (S. 127)

Pigfish, our constant companion

Der Hai wird an die Bordwand geholt (S. 129)

The shark is brought to the side wall

Am Netzabweiser wurde der Hai vorgeheißt   (S. 129)

The shark was pregiven on the net deflector

Besonders beliebt war das Würstchenschnappen (S. 130)

Sausage snapping was particularly popular

Unser „Wellenbad" am Heck (S. 131)

Our "wave pool" at the rear

Schwere Atlantikdünung – Blick nach vorn (S. 132)
Heavy Atlantic dune - look ahead

Blick nach achtern (S. 132)
Looking aft

Angespannt blickt jeder nach oben (S. 137)
Everyone is looking up tense

Als wir auftauchten, waren die Zerstörer fort (S. 138)
When we showed up, the destroyers were gone

Ein Zeuge der Schlacht im Atlantik (S. 139)
A witness to the battle in the Atlantic

Das Fischen der Boje war nicht so ganz einfach (S. 139)
Fishing the buoy was not that easy

Dann ging ich an die Karte in der Zentrale   (S. 134)

Then I went to the card at headquarters

Fieberhaft arbeitet der Funkmaat an der Taste (S. 141)

The radio operator works feverishly on the button

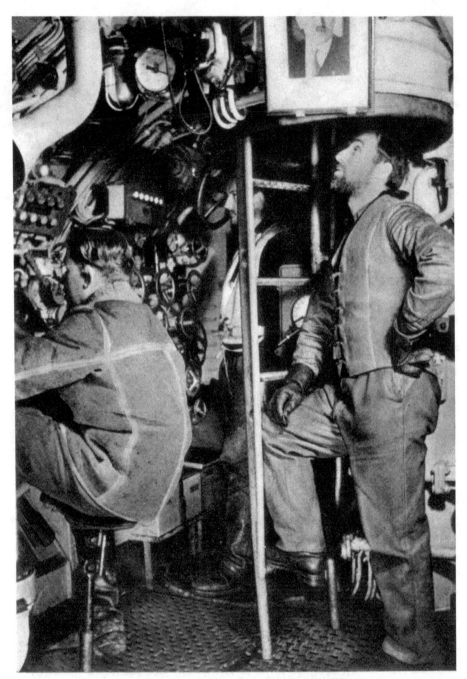

Der L. I. meldet die Tiefe in den Turm - Links ein Tiefenrudergänger   (S. 145)

The L.I. reports the depth in the tower - on the left a deep rower [depth controller?]

Unermüdlich guckt der Ausguck durchs Glas – An Brücke und Antennen bildet sich Eis (S. 147)
The lookout looks tirelessly through the glass - ice forms on bridges and antennas

. . . Nach dem Auftauchen war es weggetaut, und die Reparatur mußte schnell durchgeführt werden (S. 148)
. . . After surfacing, it was thawed away and repairs could be carried out quickly

Langsam begann das Boot sich einen festen Eispanzer anzuziehen   (S. 147

Slowly the boat started to put on a solid ice sheet

Der Kommandant trägt die Angaben in die Karte ein (S. 149)

The commander enters the information on the card

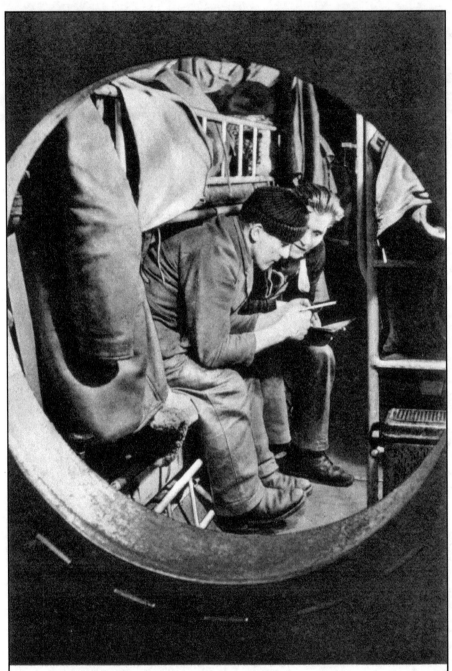

Blick in den Bugraum   (S. 150)

View of the bow area

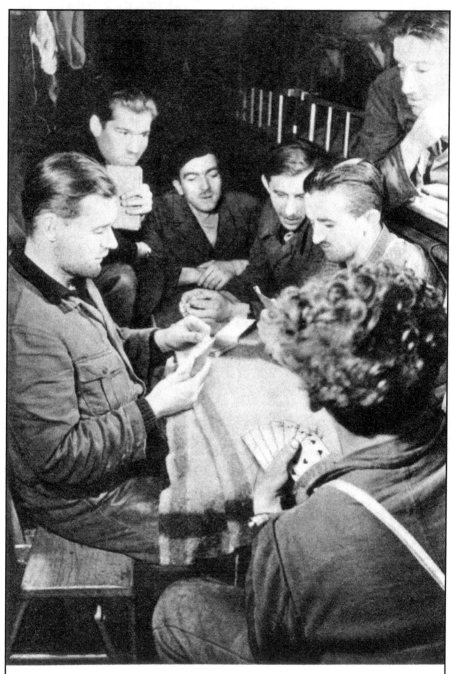

Skat im Bugraum (S. 150)

Skat in the bow area [scat is a German card game]

Mit Höchstfahrt jagte „U . . ." dem Geleitzug entgegen   (S. 150)

"U ..." chased the convoy with an ascent

Tief wühlte es sich in die See   (S. 150)

It was deep in the sea

Kleine Weihnachtsbäumchen standen auf unserer Brücke S. 168

Small Christmas trees stood on our bridge

Der Kommandeur des Patenbataillons schmückt die Bäumchen (S. 168)

The commander of the godfather battalion decorates the saplings

Blick in die Zentrale, wo der Weihnachtsbaum geschmückt wird   (S. 169

View of the headquarters, where the Christmas tree is being hung

v. Schroeter spielt die Weihnachtslieder (links im Hintergrund der Verfasser) (S. 169)

Schroeter plays the Christmas carols (on the left in the background the authors)

Ein Fähnrich verteilt die Weihnachtstüten   (S. 169

An ensign distributes the Christmas bags

In der Feldwebelmesse lesenObersteuermann und Dieselmaschinist ihreWeihnachtspost   (S. 170)

The helmsman and diesel machinist read their Christmas mail at the sergeant fair [?]

„Hannes" (links) und „Otto" backen unsere Weihnachtspfannkuchen   (S. 169

"Hannes" (left) and "Otto" bake our Christmas pancakes

Weihnachten in der Offiziersmesse – von links: Oblt. z. See Hoffmann, der Verfasser, Lt.
z. See v. Schroeter, Oblt. (Ing.) Schulz   (S. 169

Christmas in the officers' mess - from left: Lieutenant (junior grade) Hoffman, the author, Ensign
Schroeter, Lieutenant (junior grade) (engineer) Schulz

Weihnachten in der Kommandanten-Ecke (S. 170)
Christmas in the commander's corner

Der Torpedomaat stoppt die Laufzeit des Torpedos ab (S. 173)

The torpedo mate stops the torpedo running time

Der Bug guckte noch 30 m steil aus dem Wasser (S. 176)

The bow looked out of the water for another 30 minutes

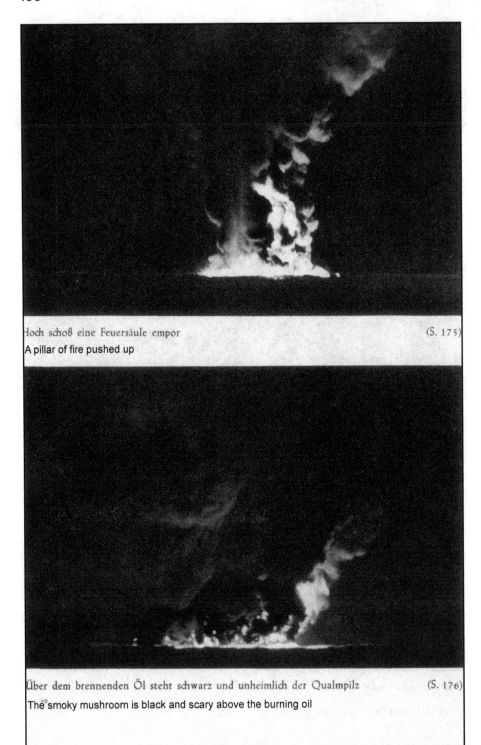

Hoch schoß eine Feuersäule empor (S. 175)
A pillar of fire pushed up

Über dem brennenden Öl steht schwarz und unheimlich der Qualmpilz (S. 176)
The smoky mushroom is black and scary above the burning oil

Kraxel" bastelt das Ritterkreuz (S. 18

"Kraxel" builds the knight's cross

Wir drehten hart ab, langsam sackt er achtern tiefer   (S. 192)
We turned hard, slowly he sank aft lower [SS *Culebra*]

Gefechtspause   (S. 192)
Battle lull [SS *Culebra*]

Deutlich sind unter dem Schornstein die Einschläge und unter der brennenden Brücke das ausgerauschte Boot zu erkennen [SS *Culebra*] (S. 192)

You can clearly see the deposit under the smokestack and the broken boat under the burning bridge

Dann gingen wir an die Boote heran (S.192)

Then we went up to the boats [SS *Culebra*]

Die Besatzung durfte das Sinken der „Culebra" sich ansehen – achtern das Geschütz   (S. 193)

The crew were allowed to watch the sinking of the *Culebra* - aft protection

Die Brücke brennt, der Bug richtet sich auf   (S. 193)

The bridge burns, the bow rises

In einer großen Rauch- und Qualmwolke versank . . .

Sank into a coarse cloud of smoke and steam

. . . die „Culebra" dann endgültig   [S. 1##]

. . . the *Culebra* then finally

Im Bugraum werden Wimpel genäht und beschriftet   (S. 196)

Pennants are sewn and labeled in the bow area

Die Wimpel werden gesetzt (S. 196

The pennants are set

Zehn Wimpel flatterten vom Sehrohr (S. 196)

Ten pennants fluttered from the periscope

Einlaufen – Von links: Oblt. z. See Hoffmann, der Verfasser, Lt. z. See v. Schroeter (S. 196)

Enter - from left: Lieutenant (junior grade) Hoffmann, the author, Ensign von-- Schroeter

Unser Turm beim Einlaufen vom Paukenschlag   (S. 196)
Our tower coming home from the bang [drumbeat]

Das Boot läuft in den inneren Hafen ein   (S. 196)
The boat enters the inner harbor

Auf den U-Booten waren die Besatzungen angetreten (S. 196)
The crews had started on the submarines

Langsam näherten wir uns der „Isère" (S. 196)
We slowly approached the *Isere*

Der Befehlshaber stand oben auf der „Isère"   (S. 196)
The commander was on top of the *Isere*

Admiral Dönitz legt mir das Ritterkreuz um   (S. 197)
Admiral Doenitz puts down the Knight's Cross

Der Glückwunsch des B. d. U. (S. 197)

Congratulations from the BdU. [Befehlshaber der Unterseeboote = Commander of U-boat HQ]

Als jüngster Ritterkreuzträger (S. 197)
schritt ich die Front der Ehrenkompanie und meiner Besatzung ab

As the youngest Knight's Cross bearer
I walked off the front of the honorary company and my crew

Guter Grund zur Freude (S. 197

Good reason to be happy

„Ikke", unser Zentraleheizer, als Mädchen für alles beim Reinschiff

"Ikke", our central heating, as a girl for everything on the reef

Das ganze Schiff war in ein Flammenmeer gehüllt   (S. 201

The whole ship was shrouded in a sea of flames

Während der Bug sich aufbäumt brennt das Öl auf dem Wasser weiter   (S. 201

While the bow is building up, the oil on the water continues to burn

Der Tanker brannte lichterloh (S. 205)
The tanker was on fire

Brennender Tanker vor der USA.-Küste (S. 211)
Die einzelnen Bunker waren in Brand geschossen

Burning tanker in front of the USA coast
The individual bunkers were set on fire

Beim Angriff am Sehrohr (S. 204)

When attacking the periscope

Im Schlauchboot wurde uns eine Kiste Eier gebracht (S. 220)

A box of eggs was brought to us in an inflatable boat

Unsere Kanone zeigte fünf versenkte Schiffe (am Netzabweiser eine Haifischflosse) (S. 220)

Our cannon showed five sunk ships (a shark fin on the net deflector)

Ich stellte dem Großadmiral meine Besatzung vor   (S. 220)
links Admiral Dönitz und der Flottillenchef Korv.-Kpt. Schütze
I introduced my crew to the Grand Admiral
On the left Admiral Doenitz and the flotilla chief Lieutenant Commander Schultze

Eigenhändig heftet der Großadmiral den Männern die E. K.s an   (S. 220)
links vom Verfasser Admiral Dönitz

The Grand Admiral hand-tacked the E. K.s to the men [E. K. = Eisernen Kreuzes or Iron Cross]
To the left of the author is Admiral Doenitz

Unser Torpedomaat hat guten Grund zu lachen, als unser Kriegsberichter Meisinger ihm hilft, das E. K. zu befestigen (S. 220)

Our Torpedo couple have good reason to laugh when our war correspondent Meisinger helps him fasten the E.K. [E. K. = Eisernen Kreuzes or Iron Cross]

Großadmiral Raeder im U-Stützpunkt (S. 220)
links Kptlt. Topp, rechts Korv.-Kpt. Merten, der Verfasser, Kptlt. Witte

Grand Admiral Raeder in the U-base
Left Lieutenant (senior grade) Topp, right Lieutenant Commander Merten, the author, Lieutenant (senior grade) Witte

Aus der Hand des Führers erhielt ich das Eichenlaub (S. 221)

I received the oak leaves from the hand of the Fuhrer [Adolf Hitler]

Langsam laufen wir in die Förde ein (S. 224)
We are slowly running into the Fjord

Der II. A. d. U. schreitet die Front der Besatzung ab (S. 225)
The second admiral of U-boat Headquarters is walking past the front of the crew [loosely]

Zum erstenmal macht das Boot wieder in der Heimat fest   (S. 225)
For the first time the boat moored back home

C5 – Norway Bound

According to an old Chinese proverb, the longest trip starts with a single step. In the case of the trip to Norway, that single step was taken by Rusty Cassway when he offered to donate the builder's plaque of the *Octavian* to the Norwegian Maritime Museum. That step set in motion a series of events that culminated in a donation ceremony that was unequaled in wreck-diving history.

This is not to say that wreck-divers had never donated artifacts before. After all, Deb Whitcraft's New Jersey Maritime Museum was filled with an abundance of artifacts – literally thousands of individual items – all of which had been donated by dedicated wreck-divers who wanted to share their historic finds with the non-diving public: people who would never see such relics in the depths of the underwater environment from which they had been rescued, cleaned, and preserved with tender loving care.

In order to attend the ceremony on Norway's Liberation Day – when the artifact was scheduled to be officially donated to the museum officials for display in the museum – Rusty organized an elaborate week-long extravaganza that straddled the formal bestowal of the builder's plaque. He also invited all his friends, dive buddies, and their significant others who wished to attend the formal celebration.

For reasons that I am unable to fathom, Rusty extended an invitation to this author. After all, my time and input in helping to identify the *Octavian* by determining the correct U-boat that sank her, and in pinpointing the location where she sank, was miniscule. Perhaps I underrate myself. A lifetime of shipwreck research gave me a perspective and a personal library that enabled me to put my finger on pertinent facts and suppositions that pointed in the right direction. I suppose that facility is worth something.

On the other hand, perhaps long-time friendship had something to do with Rusty's invitation. I first me Rusty in 1983. At that time he was 16 years old, was still in high school, was a newly certified scuba diver, and was working part time for his instructor, Evelyn Dudas, at her dive shop, called Dudas' Diving Duds. That same year, an underwater symposium was held at the Philadelphia Navy Yard. I was one of the speakers. Evie was an attendee, and she brought Rusty with her to the symposium.

Afterward, all three of us plus several other people had dinner at a restaurant that was owned by one of my dive buddies, Ed Cellini. We chose Ed's restaurant not only because he was my friend, but because he had decorated the walls with numerous artifacts that I had recovered from local shipwrecks.

The following year – on September 8 – we met again, this time aboard Bill Nagle's 35-foot-long Maine Coaster called the *Seeker*, which operated out of Brielle, New Jersey. Our destination that day was the *Ayuruoca*: a Brazilian freighter that sank on June 10, 1945, after colliding with the Norwegian motor vessel *General Fleischer*. The latter vessel survived the collision, and proceeded under her own power to New York City for repairs.

The wreck of the *Ayuruoca* lay at a depth of 170 feet. Because the hull stood upright on the muddy bottom of the appropriately named Mud Hole (the extension of the Hudson River and all the dirt and debris that floated out to sea from New York City), the main deck rose to 140 feet, and the upper levels of the wheelhouse rose twenty feet higher.

Rusty's dive buddy that day was his school chum Daniel Stegeman. They slid down the anchor line and dropped to the main deck, where they entered a corridor that lead to compartments on either side. Those compartments had suffered considerable collapse. However, by moving debris and digging through the silt, they recovered several utensils on which were stamped the crest of the shipping line: the company flag surrounded by the lettering "LLOYD BRASILEIRO · COMPANHIA de NAVEGASAO."

The purpose of my dives was to photograph the wreck – although I did manage to catch a lobster on each of my two dives. I was envious when I saw the pristine silverware that Rusty and Daniel had recovered. They split the trove equally between them. Because they had duplicate utensils, and because I had duplicate utensils that I had previously recovered from the USS *San Diego* – an armored cruiser that had been sunk in World War One after striking a German mine off the coast of Long Island, New York – Rusty offered to trade one of his *Ayuruoca* forks for one of my *San Diego* forks.

Our friendship was bonded on such an exchange.

Now Rusty made another offer that I couldn't refuse. No, he didn't put a horse's head on the pillow next to mine. Instead, he proposed to give me a roundtrip plane ticket to Norway. All I had to do was share lodging expenses with the other people on the trip. After due consideration, I accepted his offer.

Project Octavian was slated to commence on May 3, 2019.

Hail, Hail, the Gang's All Here!

The trip originated at Newark International Airport, in Newark, New Jersey. Except for me, the rest of the gang lived in New Jersey. They met at a convenient location, and traveled in one limousine. I was the only member of the group who lived in Pennsylvania – in the so-called winter wonderland known as the Poconos. Cheryl Novak, my other half, drove me to the airport, and promised to pick me up when I returned.

I arrived two hours early because I have a dread of encountering traffic or suffering a mechanical breakdown along the way. I would rather sit in the airport lounge and read a book than miss a flight. We had not designated a place to meet, so after processing my ticket with Icelandair, I hung out in the lobby. I didn't have to wait too long before the gang started to make its appearance, appearing one by one in advance of those who were dawdling with their heavy luggage.

It was like a reunion with friends whom I had not seen in a long while, especially as I had quit diving in 2011. Rusty Cassway had a big hug for me. You may recall that Mike Dudas and Tom Packer were on the momentous dive when Rusty found the builder's plaque. Tom was accompanied by his wife Kim, whom I had known since the 1980's before she and Tom had children. Mike I had known since his birth, as at that time I was close friends with his parents John and Evie. He had with him his girlfriend Liberty Belle Jay (for real). When I asked her about her curious name, she told me that her parents were "different."

John Copeland and I had been together on some long-distance dive trips, such as Nova Scotia and Newfoundland, both in Canada. I had also taken him mountain biking a couple of years earlier. Tim Terrey I met at my house in Jim Thorpe when he and Rusty visited in order to do some shipwreck research (unrelated to the *Octavian*). David Fisher I did not know; he was Rusty's business partner at Demountable Concepts. Dave was not a diver, but he was an avid photographer, of Norwegian descent, and interested in the history of World War Two.

The camaraderie that started at this meeting lasted for the entire trip, and beyond.

I had some trouble at the security check. The security guards took exception to my powdered Gatorade, which I intended to mix with Norwegian water as liquid refreshment for the week. After examining the cardboard container, a guard placed it in an appliance that looked to me like a microwave oven. He tapped a few buttons, and, as it appeared to me, nuked the powder. The Gatorade passed the test and was retrieved unburned, after which he handed the container back to me.

The guard who was assigned to me also took exception to my digital camera: a Canon EOS 5D with two lenses. He asked me to remove the lens that was on the camera so he could look inside the body. He examined both lenses visually. Then he ran a patch of cloth over the camera body, and inserted the patch into the microwave oven. I would have been worried if this had been a film camera.

Before he let me have my camera and lenses, he ran a swath over my hands and wrists and gave the swath the microwave test. Everything passed to his satisfaction.

Then he explained that he had tested me and my equipment and Gatorade for gunpowder residue. The Gatorade powder was colored pale baby blue: my favorite flavor that is called Glacier Freeze. It didn't look like any gunpowder that I had ever seen in the Army. But upon mature reflection, I acknowledged that a clever terrorist could have dyed gunpowder to match the color of Gatorade, then placed it in a Gatorade container as a way to smuggle an explosive onboard the aircraft. Then, my camera body and lenses could have been empty shells that hid a detonator or timing device.

I never would have thought of any of these shifty measures of concealment, but then I am not a terrorist with a bone to pick against non-Islamic humanity. Unfortunately, liberal tolerance does not work both ways.

A situation like this reminds me of the words of Ambrose Bierce, that sardonic author and lexicographer who, in *The Devil's Dictionary*, defined "faith" as "belief without evidence in what is told by one who speaks without knowledge, of things without parallel."

I suppose that in some twisted minds this makes me an infidel. Oh, well. Amen to that.

Ours was an overnight flight that landed in Keflavik, Iceland at 5:30 in the morning, with a two-hour forty-minute layover before our departure for Oslo, the capital of Norway. We didn't see any of the countryside; we didn't even have enough time to leave the airport. About all we could do was to have a meal. Whether it was breakfast, brunch, or a midnight snack, I never determined.

Then it was back on the plane for the next hop. We landed at Oslo at 12:30 in the afternoon. It was either too early or too late for bed, so we decided to stay awake for the rest of the day. We split into three groups: Tom and Kim to their hotel, Mike and Liberty to their hotel, and the five guys to their Airbnb (pronounced air-bee-en-bee, a take-off on B&B, which stands for Bed and Breakfast, an inn that serves breakfast to travelers after a night's lodging).

While we were unpacking and scrambling for first dibs on rooms and beds, we had a visitor from the Norwegian Maritime Museum: the director Sven Ahrens and his son. Rusty unwrapped the cloth that kept the builder's plaque from getting scratched, so that Sven could have a preview of the object whose official unveiling would transpire on Wednesday, May 8, four days hence. They became the first Norwegians to touch the plaque in 76 years.

After Sven and his son departed, with a promise to meet us for dinner, we hid the plaque under a cushion of the sofa in the living room, then spent the remainder of the afternoon in exploring that part of Oslo that catered to tourists. We meandered along the city's maritime quarter past the bulkheads that kept the water in Oslofjord from erod-ing the land. We bumped into Mike and Liberty at one point, then into Tom and Kim at another. It seemed that we all had the same idea: al-though we were exhausted from the overnight flight, it was too early to go to bed, and the only way to stay awake was to keep moving on cob-blestone streets in the brisk afternoon air.

We saw ships in the harbor such as ferry's crossing the fjord, and sailing vessels docked to the wharf. We saw neat and clean tenement housing. We saw intricate artwork painted on the buildings. We saw mobs of locals who were taking advantage of Saturday delights, but minus the pushing and shoving that you might find in an American city.

What we did *not* see was trash on the streets or gutters or walk-ways: not a speck of paper nor cigarette butt nor windblown news-papers nor soggy masses of tabloid sheets. One time we crossed paths with a street cleaner who was having a difficult time at finding trash to collect. I saw him bend over to pick up a paper patch that was no bigger than a postage stamp: likely a torn-off corner of a full sheet of paper whose owner didn't notice the wind whisking away the scrap. Oslo was the cleanest city that I have ever seen.

Our most unexpected find was a life-sized statue of Franklin Delano Roosevelt, sitting in a chair on a large granite pedestal that overlooked the harbor. Norwegians paid homage to the President of the United States for a number of reasons.

After Germany invaded Poland on September 1, 1939, thus throwing Euro-pean countries into a state of war, Roosevelt was sensitive to Norway's situation with regard to further Nazi ag-gression and military expan-sion. The initial United States Congressional stance of non-interference did not prevent Roosevelt from as-sisting beleaguered Allied nations. He was responsible for having much-needed food and supplies smuggled into Norway during the Nazi assault.

Nazi Germany's sub-sequent invasion of Norway forced the Norwegian gov-ernment to operate in exile.

King Carl Haakon VII and Crown Prince Olav Haakon retreated to London, England, while Crown Princess Martha Haakon and her three children crossed the border into Sweden, where she had been born.

It was thought by some that the Nazi's might look upon Martha's move as a violation of Sweden's neutrality. She, the children, and their household help then moved to Finland. Finland was unsettled as she was at war with the Soviet Union. Martha and her children and entourage then received an invitation from Roosevelt to live in the United States at the White House. Apparently, Roosevelt was not intimidated by the Nazis with regard to their concerns about neutrality. Martha and all remained at the White House as honored guests throughout the war. She sometimes had dinner with Roosevelt and his wife Eleanor.

Even before the Nazis commenced overt hostilities against the United States, Roosevelt initiated the Lend-Lease Act, on March 11, 1941. (See Chapter 4 for details.)

To further flaunt his stance against the Nazis with respect to U.S. alignment in the European war, on September 16, 1942, Roosevelt held an open ceremony in which he donated the newly built patrol craft *PC 467* to the Norwegian government. This patrol boat measured 175 feet in length, grossed 357 tons, and could ply the waves at 20 knots. She was armed with two 3-inch deck guns, two Oerlikon 20-millimeter cannons, two Colt 20-millimeter anti-aircraft machine guns, two depth charge throwers, and sixty depth charges. There was no doubt about where Roosevelt's allegiance lay. By donating a warship to Norway, he was figuratively thumbing his nose at Hitler.

Just in case Hitler missed his point, at the presentation ceremony, Roosevelt praised Norway's resistance movement by giving what came to be known as his "Look to Norway" speech: "If there is anyone who still wonders why this war is being fought, let him look to Norway. If there is anyone who has any delusions that this war could have been averted, let him look to Norway; and if there is anyone who doubts the democratic will to win, again I say, let him look to Norway."

Martha was in attendance at the presentation ceremony. She responded to Roosevelt's speech by saying, "The beautiful and generous words just expressed by you, Mr. President, will ultimately find their way to every Norwegian home. Yes, to everywhere on this globe where Norwegian men and women are praying and working and fighting to regard the free and happy Norway. All our deepest thanks."

The *PC 467* was rechristened the *HNoMS King Haakon VII*. With a Norwegian navy crew, she did admirable service throughout the war.

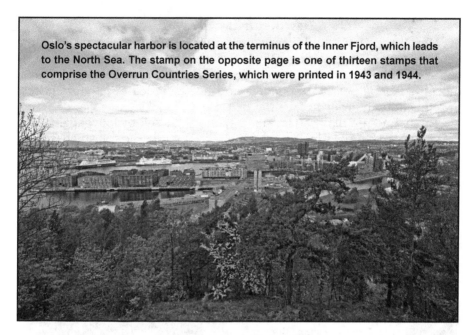

Oslo's spectacular harbor is located at the terminus of the Inner Fjord, which leads to the North Sea. The stamp on the opposite page is one of thirteen stamps that comprise the Overrun Countries Series, which were printed in 1943 and 1944.

Based at Halifax, Nova Scotia, she started her wartime career by escorting convoys across the Atlantic Ocean between Canada and England. She then did service around the British Isles. In 1943 she was transferred to St. John's, Newfoundland. From there she escorted convoys along the eastern seaboard of the North American continent, in the Gulf of Mexico, and throughout the Caribbean Sea. During this duty she traveled more than 85,000 miles while escorting seventy-nine convoys, without sustaining any accidents or serious injuries to her expatriate crewmembers.

After the capitulation of Nazi Germany, the *King Haakon VII* headed for her homeland. She docked at Kristiansand on June 26, 1945. Home at last!

Norway honored Roosevelt for all these reasons. That is why a statue of him graces the harbor in Norway's capital city.

Because Oslo is located so far north, the daylight hours extended well into what we thought should be night. We had plenty of time for more walkabout after dinner. A local grocery store enabled us to stock our temporary larder with breakfast essentials and snack food: coffee, milk, sugar, cereal, and so on. Both Rusty and Dave used a map application on their smartphones to keep us on track as we wandered along the highways and byways through town. We were surprised to learn after returning to our room that altogether we had walked a distance of eight miles.

I had no trouble sleeping that night.

Day 3, Sunday, May 5

Day 1 and Day 2 had blended together in a blur of meeting, flying, landing, flying, and touring. Day 3 arrived with the five "guys" sipping coffee in order to offset the groggies: American slang for the sluggish morning feeling before our bodies and heavy-lidded eyes commenced to rejuvenate in order to face the new day.

Rusty had not planned for us to spend the week by lollygagging. He had prepared a daily itinerary to which strict adherence was necessary. This didn't mean awakening at oh-dark-hundred, but it did mean not languishing in a bathroom that had to be shared by five men, then getting underway because there was a strict schedule to keep.

Today's first destination was a Jewish Heritage Museum called the Holocaust Center, with our 5-star tour by local guide Christine Dahl. We collected Chris (for short) at the Oslo main train terminal. She had to travel with five boisterous guys who constantly plagued her with questions. Like a true professional, she answered every question with forbearance and full knowledge of the subject matter.

The Holocaust Center, alias the Jewish Heritage Museum.

We traveled by bus. This turned out to be a bit of adventure in itself, as bus drivers do not collect money. Chris explained the way the system worked. Everyone who lived in Norway had a smartphone – and I stress the word "everyone." A person cannot live in Norway without a smart phone.

Perhaps "smartphone" is a bit of a misnomer. The device is actually a personal mini-computer that incidentally has the capability of making phone calls. If you can believe it, Norway has no bank buildings and no post offices or postal service.

Personal money accounts are held online, and banking business is done via the Internet; this means salaries, sales, loans, and so on. All letters are sent via the Internet through electronic mail service as emails. (You might recall that "email" is short for "electronic mail," the dash in the original abbreviation of e-mail having long ago been dropped.)

If you need to ship a package, you do it via a government-operated package service that maintained a kiosk in the rear of supermarkets. The government did not ship the package as it does in the States, but farms out the package to a private delivery service, the way Americans might ship a package via United Parcel Service or Federal Express Ground. Thus Norway has done away with postage stamps.

Nearly all payments are made via credit card, which deducts the payment from the buyer's online bank account, and credits the payment to the seller's online bank account. Paper bills and metal coins are still used, but lower denomination coinage has been discontinued.

The payment system made it easy for foreign tourists (such as we). I never had to exchange any American money for local currency. I used a credit card to pay for all my meals and other purchases.

To get back to the bus, where this economic diversion began, bus tickets were purchased online. Chris showed Rusty how to download the app for bus fares onto his smart phone. He then went to the bus website, input the route number for which he wanted to purchase electronic tickets, and used his credit card to pay the appropriate amount. (To simplify and accelerate the process, instead of all of us buying our own tickets, Rusty paid for all of them at once, and we reimbursed him individually.)

Chris told us that Norway was the most technologically advanced country in the world. After this brief introduction, I believed her implicitly.

Our arrival at the Holocaust Center was accompanied by jubilation. Thanks to Chris's guidance, we had reached our destination through new technological adventures. But after entering the building, jubilation changed abruptly to solemnity as we viewed the photographic displays of the haggard visages on people who were on their way to concentration camps. We listened in awe to Chris's dialogue about how the Nazi's first order of business after invading Norway was to gather local Jews for the holocaust grinding machine.

More than two thousand Jews lived in Norway at the time of the occupation. Approximately two-thirds of them escaped the fate that Hitler had in store for them. Some fled the country before the Nazi's took full control; the resistance movement smuggled some nine hundred others to Sweden and England.

Nearly eight hundred were captured by the Nazis and transferred to concentration camps. Only around thirty survived the horrors of imprisonment.

I was too overwhelmed by remorse to take photographs.

Our next stop for the day was a bit more uplifting: the Viking Ship Museum. Our guide Chris told us that she had a Ph. D in Vikinging, then went on to explain that in its broadest definition the word Viking referred to all Scandinavian explorers and wanderers, not just Norwegians as the common myth portrays. Not only did we learn about historical Vikings, but we were enthralled by actual thousand-year-old Viking ships that had been unearthed, restored, conserved, and displayed full-scale in huge rooms that had been purpose-built to house these incredible relics of Norway's past.

Next door stood the Historical Museum which, along with the Viking Ship Museum, were called collectively the Museum of Cultural History. These museums were equivalent to the Smithsonian Institution in Washington, DC (District of Columbia). On display here were extremely detailed medieval carvings, horse-drawn wagons in all their glory, royal sledges, and well-preserved household items.

The day still wasn't over. We next visited a medieval church that was known locally as a stave church. "Stave" refers to the building's post-and-beam type of construction. It looked as if the church's stout wooden beams could have supported the Brooklyn Bridge. Next to the church survived an entire Norwegian village whose stone foundations served as the bases for two-story log cabins. As we toured the village, Chris explained the details of building construction and native life in olden times.

All three of these facilities were staffed by museum personnel who, like Chris, spoke flawless English, as if English were their native tongue instead of their second language. They didn't even have an accent. There were occasional lapses when they groped for an uncommon word, which was usually a technical term that was not part of everyday usage. Otherwise, I might have been standing in any American museum or village reconstruction instead of in a Scandinavian country. This was our introduction to the people of Norway, past and present.

Day 4, Monday, May 6

There was a slight fumble in the morning due to confusion about the rental van. Rusty was supposed to meet Mike at the rental facility in order to sign the rental documents. Rusty was late, Mike was on time, so after some parlaying between the two over the phone, Mike signed the documents and drove the van to our Airbnb.

The six of us then headed along the coast on an hour-and-a-half ride to meet Bjorn Tore Rosendahl of the Peace and Human Rights Museum in Kristiansand. The scenery was picturesque as we rode through tunnels under sheer mountain prominences, where building switchback roadways would have been far more onerous than blasting through solid rock.

Bjorn led us through the new annex to the original building which, during the war, served as the Gestapo headquarters in southern Norway. Here mementoes of the Nazi invaders were kept as reminders of how the Nazis incarcerated people and tortured them for days, and weeks, even months. There seemed to be no end of the evil that Hitler's soldiers inflicted upon Norway and her citizens, and by extrapolation, upon the rest of Europe. After the tour of the chilly and chilling basement jail cells, our host provided lunch in a warm and well-illuminated conference room. I felt as if I had just left hell for heaven.

We then took a short drive to a marina where the museum was in the process of renovating a World War Two freighter called the *Hestmanden*. The steamship was not yet open for public tours, but Bjorn's position allowed him to make exceptions to the rule. Onboard, we were introduced to our female tour guide who, again, spoke perfect English without any hint of accent. When I closed my eyes and listened to her voice, I swore that I was hearing smooth traditional Midwestern speech with the barest hint of a Southern twang, topped by crisp enunciation and evident lack of slang. She spoke better English than most Americans of my acquaintance.

Bjorn then insisted that we accompany him on a short cruise in his motorboat. In the van, we followed his car along a motorway, then somehow wound up in the parking lot of a huge IKEA. I thought we were lost. As Bjorn later explained, IKEA makes some of the best baked cinnamon rolls, and he wanted to treat us to his  favorite delicacy. We then followed him into the wilderness to his "cabin." I used quotation marks because his cabin was not what Americans picture when they hear that word: a log cabin whose logs are poorly chinked, a wooden floor that creaks under pressure, and furniture that was knocked together from tree trunks and limbs. I would call his hidden abode a well-appointed cottage, whose deck overlooked the water and a multitude of islands whose bare rock offered little opportunity for vegetation to take hold.

The air was cold and the water was colder. We were all bundled up in all the outer wear that we had brought with us, plus life vests. I was on the point of shivering when it started to rain; then I went beyond that point. Nonetheless, I would not have traded that excursion among the boulders and islets for a dunk in a hot tub. Half an hour later, as we were tying the boat to the dock, the sun emerged in all its glory, and stayed unclouded until nighttime.

The drive back to Oslo was extended by a long detour around road improvement. We did not reach our Airbnb until eleven o'clock at night. A couple of the guys – I don't remember who – went out for pizza, and brought several pies to the room. We chowed down pizza like half-starved cats.

Day 5, Tuesday, May 7

This was supposed to be my favorite day: the one that I had been looking forward to the most. I can't say that I did not enjoy Norway's museums and historical background. All of that phase of the trip touched the educational side of my person. But I also possessed a strong physical side that had been manifested in diving (obviously), hiking, backpacking, canoeing (both whitewater and wilderness), rock and mountain climbing, and most recently, mountain biking. I was very much an outdoor person, so I desperately wanted to do the ten-to-twelve-mile hike in the mountains that Chris had suggested.

It was not to be. The guys got out of bed too late, lingered over their coffee too long, and moved so sluggishly in the morning that by the time Rusty got around to calling Chris to arrange for a meeting place, she said that the day was too far gone to drive to the mountains and hike the trail that she had in mind. I countered by pulling out my flashlight, and exclaiming that I wasn't afraid of the dark, but she could not stay late in the afternoon because she had another tour to guide at 4 p.m.

So Chris suggested that we meet in town and take a walk in the high park that adjoined the harbor. The nature trail was paved, and was adorned by modern art objects that she thought we would find edifying. I reluctantly yielded. But I'm still sorry that I didn't have the opportunity to hike in Norway's mountains.

The start of the trail was steep, but once we reached the higher elevation, the graveled surface leveled out and wound through a beautiful forest that was dotted with art objects that were not only enlightening, but fascinating. Many of the sculptures were molded in such a way that

Note that the direction in which the carved image faces appears to have changed with respect to my viewing position, as I moved around the block. The statue below was located near a wharf on the promenade that surrounds the harbor. The bird on the woman's head was not part of the artist's original design.

they created optical illusions whose configurations changed in relation to the onlooker's viewpoint. We stopped to goggle at each and every one.

After capturing an overview of the harbor from the heights, we skipped downhill to the van, then drove to a ski jump where downhill skiers practiced their skills at flying through the air while seat-bound spectators watched from a sunken amphitheater.

We then whisked back for a walking tour of a massive castle and its ramparts that overlooked the harbor. Part of the castle also served as the Resistance Museum. This museum highlighted the incredible efforts of the underground resistance movement that secretly fought against the Nazis during the occupation of Norway during World War Two. Chris added insightful information to what was printed on the plaques that accompanied the photographs.

After that we parted company with Chris so she could meet her afternoon tour. However, while walking to the place where the van was parked, Chris caught up with us and told us that the tour had been canceled. She had so much fun with us that she decided to accompany us to dinner. We were honored.

Tim Terrey had heard about a shopping mall vendor who claimed to serve the best chicken sandwich in the world – or so he said. I don't know if it was the best – not having tasted the chicken sandwiches that were served by her thousands of competitors – but it certainly was good and filling.

According to Rusty's and Dave's smartphone tracking application, we had walked another twelve miles while perambulating through Oslo.

Day 6, Wednesday, May 8

This was the big day. It was not Der Tag (The Day) that Hitler anticipated in Germany. Instead it was just the opposite for Norway: the anniversary and annual celebration of the end of Nazi Occupation, wich Norwegians called Literation Day. For Rusty it was the presentation of the *Octavian's* builder's plaque to the Norwegian Maritime Museum.

For the rest of us it meant dress wear for the occasion: not tuxedoes or three-piece suits, but casual shirts, pants, and coats without the full formality of ties. We also had to check out of our room. This meant packing our suitcases, loading the van, and driving to the location

Table at left: Mike Dudas, Liberty Belle Jay, John Copeland; Table behind: David Fisher, Tim Terrey, Tom Packer (Kim Packer's head is behind John Copeland's head).

Sven Ahrens introducing Rusty Cassway.

where the memorial ceremony was slated to start at 2 p.m. The day was perfect for all occasions: bright and sunny with a touch of wind, and warm enough not to require overcoats.

The location was also the site of a number of museums that focused on Norway's maritime history. We received a private tour that included the laboratory where relics that were recovered from local wreck sites were preserved in chemical baths and restored for public display. Tom and Kim Packer joined us for the tour, and we met Mike Dudas and Liberty Belle Jay shortly afterward.

A special luncheon was catered by the Norwegian Maritime Museum. The dining room was packed with our group of nine Americans, plus nearly eighty Norwegian descendants of the men who were lost on the *Octavian*. In his well-modulated voice, Rusty gave a photo presentation that explained where and how the *Octavian* sank, and showed underwater photos of the way the shipwreck looked today. He also bequeathed vials of sulfur – which he had collected from the cargo area of the wreck – to each and every descendant in attendance. Rusty received a rousing ovation from one and all in the dining room.

The descendants of the *Octavian's* sailors were incredibly grateful that the team from the United States had made this trip to Norway, to bring closure to a tragedy that had occurred seventy-six years earlier. Thelma Dahl, the great granddaughter of the *Octavian's* captain Jens L. Dahl, was moved to tears as she discussed what life was like for her grandfather, growing up without a father because he had been lost with the *Octavian*.

Next on the agenda was the celebration of the end of Nazi occupation at the War Monument, which was located on the same grounds. This was an annual event to which this year was added the official pres-

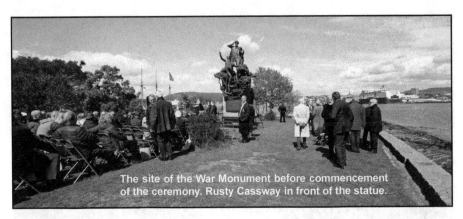

The site of the War Monument before commencement of the ceremony. Rusty Cassway in front of the statue.

entation of the *Octavian's* builder's plaque. Folding chairs were placed in front of the monument.

The ceremony started with the Norwegian Seamen Choir singing "Gud signe Norges land." Then there was a speech on behalf of the Norwegian government. This was followed by a speech that was given by Bjorn Tore Rosendahl, head of the Peace and Human Rights Centre, whom we had met at his museum in Kristiansand.

For the American contingent, the highlight of the event then occurred when Rusty gave a short speech, and officially presented the *Octavian's* builder's plaque to the Norwegian Maritime Museum.

Perhaps more pertinent to the rationale for the primary purpose of the annual celebration was the garlanding of the monument. One by one, representatives of Norwegian maritime organizations, members of

Rusty officially transferring the *Octavian's* builder's plaque to Sven.

the War Veterans Group, and widows of sailors who died in the service of their country, placed wreaths at the base of the statue.

The closing of the ceremony was announced by the Norwegian Seaman Choir when they sang the Norwegian National Anthem. Americans must understand that the end of Nazi occupation is equivalent in somber remembrance to America's Independence Day. Both events represent freedom from foreign tyranny.

After the ceremony ended, we entered the museum's banquet hall for refreshments and some less serious songs by the Norwegian Seaman Choir. Most of the descendants of the *Octavian's* crewmembers were there, so there was more time to meet and chat with them.

When the festivities were over, and we said our goodbyes to the descendants and the museum staff, we still had some time before the next stage of our Norwegian adventure. I made a beeline for the *Fram* museum across the street. I had spotted this museum upon our arrival that morning. Because I had a long and abiding interest in polar exploration, and had quite a library of contemporary books on polar expeditions, there was no way that I was leaving Oslo without seeing what artifacts the museum had on display.

The *Fram* was the name of the specially designed motorized

Tove Wefald Pedersen (Deputy Director, Norwegian Maritime Museum), and Bent Hoie (the Norwegian Health Minister) chat with Rusty and Bjorn Tore Rosendahl after the ceremony.

schooner in which Norwegian explorer Fridtjof Nansen embarked on a three-year journey across the Arctic Ocean, by letting the vessel get beset in the ice, then drifting with the pack ice until she was released into the Atlantic Ocean, in 1896. The bold endeavor was an extraordinary achievement, perhaps the most important feat being that the entire crew survived the ordeal.

It is impossible for me to describe my feelings when I pushed through the museum's doors and saw standing in front of me the biggest artifact that I have ever seen: the entire *Fram*! She measured

128 feet in length, and had a beam of 36 feet.

She stood in a building whose peaked roof was tall enough in the middle to accommodate all three masts. She was also fitted with an auxiliary engine that propelled the boat at seven knots.

Furthermore, the entire vessel was open for visitors to examine: inside and out. I visited every compartment including the engine room, where her steam engine sat spick and span, as if it had just

been delivered by the manufacturer. The entire ship was so clean and perfectly painted that she appeared to have just slipped down the ways instead of being more than a century and a quarter old.

One might think that the trip was downhill from here. One would be wrong. In fact, it was just the opposite: it was not just uphill, but way uphill.

After returning the van to the rental shop, we boarded a train for the airport, then flew to Bergen, Norway, courtesy of Scandinavian Airlines. I had the usual trouble at the security checkpoint. This time it was not because of my camera or Gatorade, but for Coca Cola. When I followed instructions and tried to dispose of the leftover coke in the waste container, the security inspector yelled at me not to pour the contents into the container. She said that I had to dump it down the drain in the restroom. A security guard escorted me partway to the restroom, to a place where he could watch me enter the restroom and not be able to leave undetected. I followed the new disposal instruction, wondering why a discard container was not available at the security station. Certainly I was not the first person in the world to arrive at the security checkpoint with a partially filled cup of soda, coffee, or water.

The guard put me back in front of the line so I did not lose my place. My camera passed inspection this time.

The flight to Bergen was short. The walk to our new Airbnb was slightly more than a mile. Both Rusty and Dave used their smartphones to show us the way. Instead of going to an office to obtain the key, Rusty had the code to a key box on the door handle. We scattered like disturbed ants at a picnic, to claim rooms and beds, then gathered in the common room where, despite the lateness of the hour, daylight filtered through the windows due to the far northern latitude.

Sharing the Airbnb with the five "guys" was Rusty's daughter Sarah. She flew in from Dublin, Ireland – where she was attending an engineering college – in order to spend some time with her father and to participate in the activities of the next several days.

Day 7, Thursday, May 9

There was no rest for the weary. In the morning we arose early for the next segment of the trip. After much coffee and a hasty breakfast on food that was left over from the Oslo phase, we walked to the train station and boarded a train that departed at 8:39 a.m.

The train transported us to a bus terminal where we went for a breathtaking ride on which the bus lost elevation faster than any of its passengers' stomachs. The downhill road was way too steep, narrow, and curvy for faint-hearted tourists from whom I heard constant cries that were not the oohs and ahs of wonder, but the muffled gasps of near and not-so-near terror.

The brakes squealed gently as the bus turned on so many hairpin switchbacks that I quickly lost count of them. The view through the window and straight down steep vertical faces brought momentary intakes of breath; occasional squeals accompanied the exhales.

The ride ended on a straightaway that terminated at a dock where we boarded a ferry for a ride through the fjords.

The only word that I can use to describe the scenery from the ferry's upper deck is "spectacular." The overcast sky and intermittent drizzle did nothing to dispel the remarkable glamor of snow-topped mountains that rose thousands of feet on both side of the fjord. Sheer rock precipices alternated with grassy and tree-covered lower slopes to create a contrast that could be appreciated from our vantage point on the water.

The ferry took us down one fjord and up another that was equally as spectacular. We passed isolated villages that were sequestered beneath towering peaks where tremendous waterfalls gushed along rocky ravines that led through tortuous passages to the sea. We spotted a group of kayakers who were paddling near shore on the placid water.

After the ferry docked, we transferred to a train that wound its way through the Flam Valley to the top of the mountains by traveling twelve miles, passing through twenty tunnels, and ascending 2,838 feet. Now we could look far downhill from a height that, due to fog, lay literally in

Snow-capped peaks tower high above the fjord.

Opposite page: Many people in this group from the train were taking selfies with the roaring waterfall in the background. Note the woman in red, about halfway up the middle cascade; she danced to music that was played over a loudspeaker.

the clouds. We saw raging rivers of snow-melt that plunged through gorges on the way to the sea in adjacent fjords.

The train stopped in order to let its passengers disembark so as to see the grandest waterfall of them all. It seemed as if everyone in a huge Asian group carried selfie sticks, so each one could take photographs of himself or herself standing in front of the waterfall in the background.

The train ride was a fitting finale. After witnessing all these sights – from the bus, from the ferry, and from the train – I didn't feel so bad about missing the hike through the woods outside of Oslo. This trip more than made up for it.

The final vehicle that we boarded that day was an electric tram that returned us to Bergen. I have a bad leg that causes chronic pain; this pain is somewhat alleviated by elevating it whenever possible. I leaned against the tram seatback, and placed my foot on the opposite seat. The conductor hit me gently on the leg and motioned for me to take my foot off the seat. This action caused a chuckle among my traveling companions. I complied, then rested my bad leg across my good one.

Later that evening, John and Tim crossed the street in front of our Airbnb to the dockside. When they looked into the crystal clear water, they spotted beach glass in the shallows. And not just a few pieces, but the mother lode of that rare and elusive beach glass that is sometimes found along eastern U.S. beaches.

Opposite page: The "beach" where glass was found. Below: One of three piles.

Beach glass consists of broken bottle shards that have been sandblasted or rolled over the rocky seabed until their sharp edges have been smoothed and the colored glass has been fogged to an artistic design of collectible and displayable chunks. Within half an hour they gathered hundreds of individual items of all sizes, shapes, and tints.

Day 8, Friday, May 10

There was still no rest for the weary. First stop on this day was the Norwegian Maritime Museum. The director gave our group a guided tour. The height of the tour occurred when he showed us public display of the Norwegian ship model collection, then offered to show us the models for which there was no space in the exhibition room. The attic was filled with dozens, perhaps scores of scale models that, like those on display, were intricately modeled from the original plans.

Suddenly, someone (I don't remember who) shouted, "Here's the *Varanger*!"

We all crowded toward the model he indicated. The name *Varanger* was indeed painted on the bow of a model that was protected inside a glass case. All of us who were divers had made numerous trips to the Norwegian tanker over the years, yet another victim of a Nazi submarine. The nighttime torpedoing of the *Varanger* was one of those rare events in which every crewmember escaped: some in lifeboats, others by leaping into the sea from which they were soon rescued by those in the lifeboats. The lucky survivors then started rowing toward shore, some twenty-eight miles away.

Neither the *Varanger* nor her cargo of fuel oil caught fire. The men who were immersed in seawater became so coated with fuel oil that Don Monchetti, the skipper of the fishing vessel *San Gennaro*, said, "all you could see were the whites of their eyes." It was daylight by the time the beleaguered merchant mariners hailed the fishing vessel. Monchetti and his crewmen pulled in their nets, secured the two lifeboats to the stern of the fishing vessel, and proceeded to tow the lifeboats toward shore.

Along the way, the *San Gennaro* encountered the fishing vessel *Eileen*. Dominick Constantino, skipper of the *Eileen*, took charge of one of the lifeboats. The small flotilla then proceeded to Townsend's Inlet,

New Jersey, which they reached at 9:30 a.m.

The survivors were taken to the Townsend's Inlet Lifeboat Station, where they were turned over to the U.S. Coast Guard. The Norwegian sailors were kept incommunicado throughout the day and evening, until they could be debriefed by officers of Naval Intelligence. In the mean time they received medical attention from Dr. Alexander Stuart. Some of the men were so thickly covered with oil that the doctor had to bathe them in kerosene.

The Coast Guard appealed to the townspeople for warm clothing and shoes. "The local Red Cross led in the response and assistance also came from near-by seaside points. Arrangements were made . . . to house the survivors in the basement of the St. Joseph Roman Catholic Church, where forty cots were set up."

For the crew of the *Varanger* there was humanity and a somewhat happy ending, instead of agony, death, and an unknown grave.

I told the guys (and gal; Sarah was with us) that I had once been on a trip to the *Varanger* with a British diver who pronounced the name as Var-ang'er (with a hard g) instead of the way we Americans pronounced it, as Var'an-jer. But what do the Brits know about pronunciation of the English language?

Next stop was a local dive shop. Rusty made an appointment to meet the owner in order to learn what kind of scuba diving was available in Bergen. There was no wreck-diving, only diving in rivers close to shore where the water wasn't too deep.

The following stop wasn't so much a stop as much as it was a browse along the harbor where vendors greeted tourists who disembarked from ferries in order to shop, eat, and tour Bergen. Most of us took the opportunity to purchase gifts for the folks back home.

During this walk along the Bergen waterfront we met Tom and Kim, plus Mike and Liberty. Because the entire crew was together, this seemed like the perfect time to say a few words over the ashes of our most beloved and revered friend, Bart Malone, acknowledge his absence by a moment of silence, then spreading his ashes in the cold waters of the harbor.

Bart's mortal remains had been separated into several packets so that he could be spread far and wide over the world that he adored so much. The previous year, John Copeland and I had been on Gene Peterson's dive trip to St. John's, Newfoundland, where we let the wind blow his ashes over Bell Island Sound. Now we repeated the act over Bergen's harbor. As I wrote on my Facebook page after Bart's tragic demise from natural causes:

In Memoriam: Bart Malone
Yesterday – January 13, 2018 – a memorial service was held for Bart Malone. I attended but did not have the opportunity to delivery my eulogy. So I am printing it here for my Facebook

friends. Feel free to pass it along.

I first met Bart in the mid-1970's. At that time, Norman Lichtman – owner of The Dive Shop of New Jersey and a certified scuba instructor – was expanding his services by offering boats to take divers to local shipwrecks. On weekends he was so busy certifying new divers in quarries that he could not also manage the charter side of the business. He needed dive masters to handle that aspect of the dive shop.

Norman invited Bart and me to charter boats, sign up divers, and go on the trips to act as safety divers. Bart and I worked together as dive masters for the next eleven years. We took turns making the tie-in dives, and untying the hook after the last diver was out of the water. In between we offered advice about the wrecks, signed logbooks, and made occasional rescues. In accordance with the latter, one of us always had to be dressed in a wetsuit or drysuit, ready to jump into the water at a moment's notice.

Eventually I had to move on in order to dive elsewhere along the eastern seaboard and survey wrecks for my Popular Dive Guide Series. But Bart and I remained friends and dive buddies, and went on numerous dive trips together throughout succeeding years, and decades.

As we got older, we starting discussing what was going to happen to our artifacts after we left this mortal coil. At that time, no maritime museums would accept or display artifacts that had been recovered by wreck-divers. In my will, I appointed Bart as the executor of my artifacts and nautical library. His responsibility was to hold onto my "stuff" until he could find a place to display or donate it.

I then told Bart that we could no longer dive together. He asked why. I said, "Because now you have a vested interest in my demise."

But we continued to dive together anyway, although I kept a sharp lookout over my shoulder when we were both in the water at the same time. Only kidding. I trusted Bart implicitly.

Bart had a habit of recovering "artifacts" that no one else would bother to recover; artifacts that appeared to be junk that no one would want to keep or display. In his honor, this kind of relic was called a "bartifact."

Yet there was a method to his seeming madness for ugly and useless trinkets. For example, one time he recovered a square chunk of steel. Everyone on the boat laughed at him. But, he explained, it was the door of a safe. Everyone still laughed. They kept laughing until he scraped the encrustation off the inside of the door and uncovered 83 coins of various denominations from different countries. This incident proved that Bart had

methods that differed from those of other divers, and that sometimes his methods yielded true artifacts that were worth the
time and effort that were expended on recovering them.

In the more than forty years that I have known Bart, never
did a cross word pass between us. This was not because we
were friends, but because Bart . . . was Bart.

We should remember Bart not only because of what he accomplished as a diver, but for the kind of person he was.
Throughout his life Bart touched many people. I am proud to
be one of those he touched. I miss him dearly.

Bart's memory will
exist in our hearts
for as long as we
shall live. Hail, Bart.

After paying our
respects to our de-
ceased fellow diver,
we headed for the
hills – again: this
time on a tram,
called a Funicular,
which climbed a
track to the top of
the mountain whose

Bart (right) prepares to dive on the *Monitor* with Gene Peterson (middle). and Dallas LaCrone (left).

base served as Bergen's northern city limits. From the summit we had
a nearly all-around view of the city, the harbor, and the surrounding
mountains.

Instead of taking the tram back to town, Rusty, John, and I decided
to hike down the trail that descended the eastern slope of the mountain. I had forgotten to bring my hiking pole or walking stick that day,
so Rusty made one for me by trimming a fallen limb to the proper
length. He didn't want me to stumble and break my leg again.

We started in the woods where we danced with a small herd of feral
but friendly goats. They didn't balk at being touched or petted; none of
them tried to butt me with their horns when I mingled in their midst.

Halfway down the mountain we crossed the tram track, so we
waited and waved to the rest of our group as they passed under the
trail. Soon we encountered a residential area where cement roads and
sidewalks blended with the rocky substrate, and where single family
dwellings were nestled together as if they were boulders adorning the
landscape.

Farther along we reached a small kiddy playground complete with
an eighty-foot-long metal conduit that was in essence a covered sliding
board. We took turns sliding through the polished aluminum tube.

We finally made it to ground level. Rusty used his smart phone to plan a route to the Airbnb. We could have taken a bus or a cab because we were close to a terminal, but we felt like enjoying the fresh air, so we walked.

The whole gang then met for an impromptu dinner at an outdoor restaurant. The air was nearly freezing, but the waitresses provided blankets and gas heaters to help keep us warm. I was wrapped like a moth in a cocoon.

We arrived at the Airbnb after walking twelve miles throughout the day.

Day 9, Saturday, May 11

This was our final day in Norway. John and Tim collected some more beach glass, but the pickings were not as good as they had been on their first venture; they had picked over the good stuff, and the waves and tide had not yet had time to replenish the supply.

We packed our suitcases and took a taxi van to the airport. The biggest event for me was that I had no trouble in going through the security check. I had consumed all my Gatorade, and my camera held no interest to security personnel for tourists who were leaving the country.

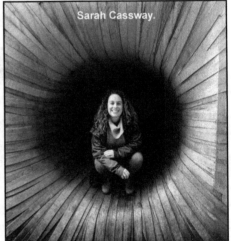

Sarah Cassway.

Sarah was with us because she was flying back to Dublin. The two couples were also with us: Tom and Kim, Mike and Liberty.

Again we had a layover in Iceland. Nothing untoward happened. We had a safe and boring flight to Newark. Cheryl was waiting for my arrival. The rest of the gang boarded a limousine. We all returned to our respective homes.

My only regret was that the group could not have stayed together longer for other wonderful adventures and continued camaraderie. After all, other shipwrecks were waiting to be discovered, explored, and identified.

The Norway trip reminded me that the most important part of wreck-diving was not the shipwrecks that I dived, nor the pictures that I took, nor the artifacts that I recovered, but the people I met along the way. Some of them were loved ones, others were long-time dive buddies, still others were newfound friends (both Norwegian and American). All were now embedded in my memory with wonderful feelings of fondness, along with the exquisite time that we had shared.

The greatest gifts in life are love and friendship.

In front of the Jewish Heritage Museum, which houses the Holocaust Center, stands a mirror that measures three stories in height and a couple of dozen feet in width. From left to right: John Copeland, Rusty Cassway, Dave Fisher, our guide Christine Dahl, the author (behind the camera, as usual), and Tim Terrey.

On a museum tour prior to the presentation of the *Octavian's* builder's plaque. Left to right: Kim Packer, Dave Fisher, Rusty Cassway, Tom Packer, John Copeland, Tim Terrey, and a museum guide.

The Popular Dive Guide Series

Shipwrecks of Maine and New Hampshire
Shipwrecks of Massachusetts: North
Shipwrecks of Massachusetts: South
Shipwrecks of Rhode Island and Connecticut
Shipwrecks of New York
Shipwrecks of New Jersey (1988)
Shipwrecks of New Jersey: North
Shipwrecks of New Jersey: Central
Shipwrecks of New Jersey: South
Shipwrecks of Delaware and Maryland (1990 Edition)
Shipwrecks of Delaware and Maryland (2002 Edition)
Shipwrecks of the Chesapeake Bay in Maryland Waters
Shipwrecks of the Chesapeake Bay in Virginia Waters
Shipwrecks of Virginia
Shipwrecks of North Carolina: from the Diamond Shoals North
Shipwrecks of North Carolina: from Hatteras Inlet South
Shipwrecks of South Carolina and Georgia

Shipwreck and Nautical History

Andrea Doria: Dive to an Era
Deep, Dark, and Dangerous: Adventures and Reflections on the Andrea Doria
Great Lakes Shipwrecks: a Photographic Odyssey
The Great Navy Wreck Scam
The Fuhrer's U-boats in American Waters
Ironclad Legacy: Battles of the USS Monitor
The Kaiser's U-boats in American Waters
The Lusitania Controversies: Atrocity of War and a Wreck-Diving History (Book One)
The Lusitania Controversies: Dangerous Descents into Shipwrecks and Law (Book Two)
The Nautical Cyclopedia
NOAA's Ark: the Rise of the Fourth Reich
Paukenschlag, Hardegen, and the SS Octavian
Shadow Divers Exposed: the Real Saga of the U-869
Shipwreck Heresies
Shipwreck Potpourri
The Shipwreck Research Handbook
Shipwreck Sagas
Stolen Heritage: the Grand Theft of the Hamilton and Scourge
Track of the Gray Wolf
The $25 Dollar Wreck of the Robert J. Walker
Underwater Reflections
USS San Diego: the Last Armored Cruiser
Wreck Diving Adventures

Dive Training
Primary Wreck Diving Guide
Advanced Wreck Diving Guide
The Advanced Wreck Diving Handbook
Ultimate Wreck Diving Guide
The Technical Diving Handbook

Nonfiction
The Absurdity Principle
Lehigh Gorge Trail Guide
Lehigh River Paddling Guide
Wilderness Canoeing

Science Fiction
A Different Universe
A Different Dimension
A Different Continuum
Entropy (a novel of conceptual breakthrough)
A Journey to the Center of the Earth
The Mold
Return to Mars
Second Coming
Silent Autumn
Subaqueous
Tesla and the Lemurian Gate
The Time Dragons Trilogy
    A Time for Dragons
    Dragons Past
    No Future for Dragons

Sci-Fi Action/Adventure Novels
Memory Lane
Mind Set
The Peking Papers

Supernatural Horror Novel
The Lurking: Curse of the Jersey Devil

Vietnam Novel
Lonely Conflict

Videotape or DVD
The Battle for the USS Monitor

Visit the GGP website for availability of titles:
http://www.ggentile.com

CPSIA information can be obtained
at www.ICGtesting.com
Printed in the USA
LVHW050252191120
672010LV00006B/288